ORKNEY DAYS

Orkney Days

An Island Life

CHRISTINE MUIR

ORIGIN

This edition first published in 2025 by
Origin, an imprint of
Birlinn Limited
West Newington House
10 Newington Road
Edinburgh
EH9 1QS

www.birlinn.co.uk

First published in book form in 1986 by
The Scotsman Publications Ltd

ISBN: 978 1 83983 094 5

British Library Cataloguing-in-Publication Data

A catalogue record for this book is available
from the British Library

Designed and typeset by Lexis Books

Papers used by Birlinn are from well-managed forests and other responsible sources.

MIX
Paper | Supporting responsible forestry
FSC® C011748

Printed and bound by Ashford Colour Ltd, Gosport

To Ena

Contents

Introduction

'All we have is every day,' the designer Terence Conran once mused ... and the same ethos informs the wondrous prose of Christine Muir.

The Orkney-based writer is among my journalistic heroes: George Orwell inspired me to write; Ian Jack inspired me to write better; and Christine Muir showed me that memorable writing need not deal with momentous events. Her accounts of North Ronaldsay's passing seasons are remarkable not just for their luminous descriptions, but also because everything they record occurred within three miles of the writer's home.

Twelve years have passed since my daughter and I – holidaying nearby – cycled to the Muir family home one sunlit afternoon: the ocean's roar ringing in our ears; its scent mingling with clover; a gulp of swallows darting before us.

It is often said you should never meet your heroes, but to step inside the croft at Garso was to enter a world I first read about three decades before as a journalism student 300 miles to the south.

Those marvellous pieces of reportage, full of light and life – written by someone I had never met, about a place I had never visited – seemed at once familiar; soothing somehow. It appears I was not alone. 'One man wrote to tell me he had read it aloud to a friend who was seriously ill in St Petersburg, to comfort him,' Christine recalls. 'Perhaps there is something calming about describing a way of life that seems reassuring in a scary world … although when I reread it, there is plenty of shivering in the cold!'

Such constant chittering is understandable, given the climate of Orkney's most northerly isle. Extreme weather is a motif running through *Orkney Days* – a collection of weekly columns written for *The Scotsman* from 1976 to 1986 and republished here with eight pieces not included in the original book.

The day before we visited Garso, Christine's brother-in-law had taken us to the top of the island's lighthouse – the tallest on British soil. Gripped by fear, I clutched the guardrail, battered by a northerly wind and awed by the power of the sea. North Ronaldsay is not for the faint hearted.

Danger lurks, even in the benignly titled 'Scented summer days', where arctic terns have a sentry posted near the five-barred gate which leads out on to the shore. Almost instantly the squadrons take off and begin their attack: 'Several times they have managed to get near enough to draw blood,' writes Christine, 'but it saves time to go along the shore so that it is better to risk the attack.'

Such stoicism has hints of the hardiness found in Alasdair Macleod's magnificent short stories set on Canada's Cape Breton coast, but it draws its inspiration from closer to home. 'I love the writing of Alison Uttley,' says Christine. 'My mother gave me *A Country Child* when I was eight, and those descriptions of life on a Derbyshire farm resonated with me – lyrical, yet honest about difficult times; descriptive but never tedious.'

Farming has changed out of all recognition since the pieces were written; so much so that the book now reads like a historical document. 'Time to sow' might easily have been penned by the Venerable Bede, far less fifty years ago

'I only wrote for my own and the family's interest,' says Christine, 'not as a record of any kind.' Stories were typed on a second-hand Olivetti and despatched by post. 'There was no editorial brief. I was simply asked to record what was happening, but I never wrote about other people, or sensitive subjects – only about ourselves, the croft and nature.' For all of the beautifully rendered accounts of a fragile landscape, hearth and home are at the heart of *Orkney Days*.

There have been huge shifts in the island's way of life since *Orkney Days* was written, and the demographic has changed significantly. 'The numbers of those whose families have lived here for generations has declined and more people have moved here, bringing many benefits, keeping the school open, and ensuring other advances. But there is an inevitable sea change too – the erosion of dialect, oral history, and traditions. These are priceless and worthy of respect.'

Not unlike the writings of Christine Muir, in fact. Until now, copies of *Orkney Days* had been, to use a farming analogy, as rare as hen's teeth, and to be greatly treasured. My own copy rests between Ian Jack's masterful

Before the Oil Ran Out and George Orwell's imperious *The Road to Wigan Pier* on our bookshelf; quietly holding its own, at ease in such exalted company.

Ronald Kerr

Note: This Introduction is based on an article which appeared in *The Scotsman*, 14 October 2024.

Ronald Kerr has been a journalist for more than forty years. As well as having written for several weekly and daily newspapers, he has worked in the press offices of the National Galleries of Scotland, the National Museums of Scotland and the University of Edinburgh.

Preface to the 2025 edition

LOOKING BACK at the sixty-three years I lived in North Ronaldsay, I feel as though the circle of life has turned, bringing me back to where I started. A newly married twenty-one-year-old moving from Edinburgh to what was then a remote crofting community, it was a difficult adjustment. It took many months before I could get used to the silence, the huge skies, the tight community, and the isolation.

It's strange how the threads of lived experience seem to weave together to make a pattern. As the stepdaughter of a North Ronaldsay man, I knew a bit about the island. Having been a student nurse helped me with skills for coping with the realities of such a life. The dialect, traditions, and culture gave me great respect for the community. Prolonged stays on a family farm had taught me to milk, rear calves, and probably led me to this path.

We loved having the children and watching them grow. Having a B and B with visitors from many countries meant they were constantly meeting people. Going to a small island school, and living on a croft, growing up with grandparents and other relatives, speaking the dialect, has been a great asset, teaching self-reliance as well as many invaluable life skills.

A small population meant that births and deaths affected everyone. A new life was greeted with joy. Grief at a death was shared, comfort, help and support freely given, and everybody attended a funeral – until recently a walking one – involving the whole island community.

Oral history was fascinating in its detail and scope. Shipwrecks, smuggling, witchcraft and superstition were discussed, as well as genealogy, and much of the relevant language was still rooted in Old Norse, such as *fryteriwark* for the occult.

Not all about island life was good. Having to part with your family at the age of eleven or twelve to go to the school hostel on the Mainland was very tough – for me the worst aspect – and they got home for only one weekend per term. Fog often meant even that was unpredictable. I missed my relatives and friends very much, and that was very difficult.

At first there was a ferry only fortnightly, bringing freight, and often that became three weeks because of weather. But it was just the way it was, and everyone was stocked up with essentials. Baking was done every day; bread from the bakery came only with the steamer. The post boat came three times a week.

Although isolation has drawbacks, anything is possible. I was able to study for three degrees and qualify as an associate lecturer with the Open University. Writing for *Farmers Weekly* and *The Scotsman* throughout the seventies, eighties and nineties has made us so many friends. It was a joy to record our daily lives.

North Ronaldsay has changed radically. As more and more people have moved in, the demographic has altered and the dialect and history are being lost, but change is inevitable, and the future depends on it. Since my husband Tommy died last year, I can no longer live on the croft and am back in Edinburgh. Ironically, the educational system in the islands ensured that all our family qualified for careers on the mainland or abroad. But growing up there has given them strength and stability as well as many skills, and a closeness which is invaluable.

I have many happy memories of the island: bringing cows home in the quiet evenings, births of calves and lambs, hatching chicks, the thousands of daffodils along the verges, the swallows returning every spring. Most of all, the neighbours who brought cakes straight out of the oven, others who often brought vegetables and fresh fish to the door, a neighbour who unfailingly knitted jumpers for all the children every Christmas. Kindness was reciprocal, and in times of trouble people helped each other as one big family.

There were many happy times, and many sad times. But the thread which runs through the pattern of life has always been love.

Christine Muir
Edinburgh, July 2025

Preface

THESE short pieces have all been published previously in *The Scotsman*, over the last ten years. They were begun as a kind of diary, a record of what it has been like to live in a small island, during the years when our family was growing up, in stormy winters and warm, sunny summers. The years chase each other so fast that it is easy to forget the hours and days which make our lives, the starry skies of winter, the mists of May, the flocks of starlings wheeling in symmetry, and the swans with their haunting call and beating wings, as they come in to land on the loch.

In these years there have been many changes. The binders are fewer, bere corn is no longer grown, and the fields of golden stooks, the crown of the harvest, are giving way to bales of hay, and silage pits. There are different breeds of cattle now; the black Aberdeen-Angus is outnumbered by Hereford and Charolais. The coming of Loganair at the end of the sixties changed all our lives for the better, and continues to benefit us in many ways. Hydro-electricity has brought us tremendous improvements, in the last three years.

But the seasons still come and go in their accustomed pattern, bringing birth and death to the island, sowing and harvest, lambing and shearing, dyke repairs and byre work. The cattle are turned out in spring, and calves race across the fresh young grass, and seals call to each other on the skerry. The lighthouse shines out every night at sunset, as it has done for more than a hundred years, and when the dark of winter comes down from the north, and storms and gales destroy the dykes, and rain lashes across the island, the thick walls of the houses keep in the warmth of the fire.

It has been a privilege and a joy to have lived in North Ronaldsay for the last twenty-five years, and to have been able to watch our family growing up. No matter what changes the future may bring, we are lucky to have had these island years to remember.

Christine Muir,
North Ronaldsay, 1986

Turning another page of the calendar

HERE in North Ronaldsay there are no flame-coloured carpets of crunchy leaves, or ripe apples and pears; no shiny conkers for small boys to play with, just a gradual fading of green through gold to the leached greys and browns of winter.

In the early autumn morning, the rocks outside the encircling dyke are covered with the delicate tracery of spiders' webs. In the pools left by the outgoing tide are shells, tiny convolutes and whorls as bright as flowers, glistening wet. Scarlet, tangerine, pale pink, primrose, amber and peach, dark blue mussels and pearly ribbed cowries lie hidden among the drifting green weed. A coven of cormorants shuffle and flap bat wings on a headland.

The harvest is late here, and until September the silver sheen of oats and the prickly tassels of bere bend in the wind, sometimes driven down by rain. In North Ronaldsay, where the old rig system still exists, combine harvesters would be a problem to operate.

The harvest field is still a lively, noisy place, with the whirr of the power-driven binder, two working the machinery, and two or more stooking, eight sheaves to a stook in a field of ley oats, six for bere. Children's bare brown legs are stubble-scratched, and fingers are blistered by the tarry binder twine. Shock-headed sheaves scatter rain water on our feet. Children play hide-and-seek among the stooks, make houses in the sheaves, and run down to the dyke to watch the seals sleeping on the rocks.

Long ago, the last sheaf was fastened up inside the barn, to bring luck to next year's harvest, perhaps a survival of the corn maiden. The last person to finish harvesting was called 'drulty at the gate', but although this has been forgotten in its original context, a child who is a slow eater and last at the table is called drulty.

Silage is replacing cereal crops here, but the fields of golden stooks are beautiful in their contrast of colour and symmetry of line, against the green pastures. It is not very long since the days of the scythe.

When the stacks are built, there is a great feeling of relief. The rhubarb patch has to supply all of the jam for winter. Rich and dark, fragrant with cloves or ginger, it bubbles in the big preserving pan on the range. The last green tomatoes are made into chutney, and onions and shallots dry in the draughty barn. In the stackyard, an ancient caraway plant shakes off its crop of seeds for carvie biscuits and seed cake, and red cabbage. Before the last stack is built in October, the lamp is lit at teatime. Only the potato harvest is left, and soon the dark of winter will catch up with us.

Autumn is a misty season, and on still evenings a milky white fog creeps in from the sea, thick and swirling. The grass is wet, and a startled snipe rises suddenly at the approach of footsteps. The air is damp and salty, and in the distance, a huge liner sails past, pale lights faintly shining. The island seems to be floating in silvery whiteness.

Inside, the kitchen is warm, and the red glow of the fire lights up the room, shining on the dresser with its cups and plates, and on the books on their shelves. We draw the curtains, and shut out the night with its shadows. It is time to turn another page of the calendar. Harvest is over, and winter has crept up silently, like a ghost over the bare fields.

Seal song

EVERY morning when I get up early and look out at the sea from the upstairs window, I see more than two hundred seals in the bay. They turn somersaults, lie on their backs in the water, flapping a lazy flipper, or bob up suddenly, whiskers dripping, like a rather pompous elderly gentleman taking an early dip.

Seals are part of our life. The people of North Ronaldsay are called selkies by the rest of Orkney. Seals are all round the island, but especially on Seal Skerry, where they have their pups, and congregate for great seal conventions and singing rallies.

When the sea haar rolls in, damp and amorphous, the seals begin their strange music, high-pitched and eerie, echoing out of the mist, and blending with the gentle splash and ripple of waves on the shingle. Their voices have a curious human quality, disembodied and far off.

When I go to fetch the cow home for milking, my feet wet from the soaking grass and marsh marigolds, it is strange to hear the seal song in the silence, with the muffled boom of the foghorn diminishing into the milky white vapour.

Because there is no shooting or culling here, the seals have little fear of human beings, and come in close to the shore. When our four children paddle in the sea, a solitary seal keeping an indolent eye open for anything curious or interesting soon drums up a few friends and relatives, by some mysterious underwater signal, and heads begin to appear all round. They swim in, and follow the splashing children all the way along the beach and back, keeping pace, and watching intently.

One night when I was taking a short cut along a sandy white bay, I came round a dune and saw a large seal only four feet away. He was completely unaware of any stranger, and I could see the beads of water shining on his sleek, speckled fur, and his sharp teeth as he opened his mouth to yawn sleepily. He scratched himself with a flipper, and rolled over on his side like a dog stretching out. He snuffled and grunted, and shook the water from his head. Eventually he spotted me, and quickly sidled down the beach and into the water.

The seals used to provide lamp oil and pelts long ago, and figure in legends and songs, like 'The Great Selkie of

Sule Skerry'. Even in this island, there was said to be a man who met a seal maiden dancing on the beach, and stole her sealskin, thus capturing her for his wife. She brought her sea cows with her, and bore seven children. Eventually, however, she found her skin hidden above the lintel of the door, and escaped back to the sea, calling her cows to follow her.

Down near the pier there is always a large colony, sleeping on the rocks and sand when the tide has ebbed, or basking in the sun in summer. They are beautiful to watch. Occasionally a baby seal is stranded up on the rocks, and lost by his mother, and he is left there alone and hungry, until hopefully she manages to retrieve him at the flood tide.

Seals are not liked by fishermen. They eat large quantities of fish, damage nets, and get in the way of creel ropes. But they are a natural part of our environment, as much as the birds, and their beauty and grace fascinate us as they splash and roll in the sea. We are lucky to live so close to this elusive creature of myth and superstition, the pinnipede with at least one flipper in mankind's door.

Merry dancers

THE merry dancers were swaying across the sky last night, to their own esoteric music, pale diffuse streamers shot with shimmering shafts of brilliant green. Sometimes in frosty weather it is easy to imagine that we can hear their thin high crackle in the silence, as we stand shivering, looking up at the vast moving curtains of light. It is strange that there seem to be so few superstitions concerning aurora borealis, for they are an eerie, awe-inspiring sight, sometimes red and green, sometimes silvery white, like slivers of ice dancing across the sky.

With no warm glow from street lamps, or intervening hills to blot out the horizon, the island is like a ship floating between dark sea and bright sky, with the moon carving a path through the water. Orion rises slowly out of the east, and moves steadily southwards, steel-green Rigel and starry belt glittering, followed by huge Sirius the dog, loping up out of the darkness. Planets cross the sky in pre-programmed formation, Jupiter with his moons, fiery Mars, Saturn with his icy rings, and more beautiful than all the rest, Venus, morning and evening star, first to shine clear and peaceful in the west.

Children quickly learn to recognise the Plough, or Charlie's Wain, Castor and Pollux the shining Twins, the

Bull with his angry red eye, Cassiopeia's silver throne, and the Seven Sisters of the Pleiades. Even the names are enthralling: Antares, Aldebaran, Arcturus and Altair. The wide sweep of the Milky Way is like an eternal spiral, with so many stars that they dazzle us. Shoals of shooting stars drift downwards in an arc, like the souls of the dead and unborn. Sometimes strange flickering hairst blinks scatter across the night sky in late autumn. With the outside lights of barn and byre switched off, the feeling of being swept along in the endless movement of the galaxies leaves us dizzy and breathless, searching for the Andromedan Nebula, two million light years away, the furthest the eyes can see into space.

The feeling is intensified by the smallness of the island, and the sound of the sea all around. In a city there are always neighbours' lighted windows, the lights of buses and cars. Here, only the lighthouse cuts a wide swathe across the sleeping fields, a golden beam which leaves the dark crofts even darker with its passing.

Often satellites pursue an apparently erratic course, so difficult to follow that we have to stand and watch intently for some time, before their imperceptible movement can be traced among the stars. The moon is so close to the earth that its craters are visible, and its light is bright enough to read by. No wonder that people used to visit each other when the moon was up, and that it was symbolic, bringing good luck to those who married with a waxing moon and a flowing tide.

We lean against the haystack, out of the wind, and watch the slow procession of the constellations across the sky. The night with its coldness and brilliance is part of winter's magic, slowing down the rush of daily life, and bringing tranquillity and peace.

Winter comes with a blast

WINTER has come with a blast straight from the polar icecap. When the cattle are being taken in for the winter, we really know what it means to live so far north. The salt spray stings our eyes and makes our ears ache, and the bitter cold blows straight through duffel coats and anoraks. The cows know that the byres mean comfort and warmth, and only the calves born outside in summer are wary and afraid to go inside with their mothers. It takes time and patience to get them in without any fuss and noise. The dark clouds race across the moon, and the stirks run round the field bellowing, excited by the activity. Eventually, cows and calves are all inside, and the doors shut.

Washing clothes is a misery at this time, although it is much easier than it used to be when the children were babies, and all the water was heated on the top of the old black range. Everything had to be washed by hand, and rinsed in cold water. Hanging clothes out is difficult, for they slap and twist. I am halfway through yet another set of storm pegs, the only ones strong enough to keep towels on the ropes, and even then they are often ripped off and torn away by the wind. Sometimes I peg them to the stack nets, where they can dry without being blown away.

Fingernails hurt, especially when they begin to thaw out, and have to be held under the cold tap until the feeling comes back. When storms combine with low temperatures, cold sores come back and chilblains itch, and there are frost hacks on heels and fingers. I get so sleepy in winter – perhaps hibernation is the answer. In summer the island looks beautiful, green grass, white sand, blue sea. The long light of the northern latitude gives an illusion of peace, but it has to be paid for by the dark side of the year.

At night the noise of sea and storm is often deafening, as the television aerial screams and whistles, and every door and window creaks and groans like a ship in a gale. Outside, the gusts drag the breath from your throat, leaving lungs compressed against ribs, and knocking you sideways. The storms blow down whole sections of sea dykes like dominoes, and the sheltering sheep are washed away into the tide. Waves and spume come pouring in through the breach, seaweed hangs from the stacks, fish boxes and floats are thrown in on the grass. The most frightening storm I have seen was last November, when the sea came through the dyke into the stackyard. Usually the energy of the waves is dispersed when they strike the rocks below the house.

Winter is not all storms and sleet. There are days when the north wind is silent, and the sea is quiet. The rugs can be hung out on the garden wall, the doors and windows opened to let in the fresh cold air, and there are no muddy footprints to mop up. The thick encrustation of salt can be washed off the window panes, and there is a breather before the glass begins to fall again.

There is time for hobbies, or for knitting for the Isle of Sanday Knitters, a co-operative which employs many of the women. A large box of packs of wool and patterns comes by steamer, and is divided up among the knitters, then the completed articles are collected, noted down, and repacked for shipping to Sanday. The work is interesting and varied, and especially good for the elderly, because it is so creative and therapeutic, as well as an activity which keeps fingers supple.

Some people have special hobbies, like the retired crofter who paints sailing ships on translucent glass fishing floats. They are perfectly round, sometimes pale green, or a faint, clear pink, or dark green. Ships in full sail, each with a figure-head, are painted in perfect perspective, with some of the crew on deck, billowing round a perpetual ocean of glass. Each ship is accurate in detail, an actual vessel flying her company flag, name and date known.

The labrador is stretched out on the rag rug at the fire, sound asleep, chasing a dream rabbit through summer fields. The children are sleeping in their wood-lined rooms, pine once salvaged from a shipwreck. The coffee pot keeps hot on the range, and the clock ticks quietly, but outside in the dark the storm rises, sending a milk-pail rattling across the yard, and the sea roars and boils as it seethes in below the dyke.

Fancy work for idle hands

WE HAVE a 1902 copy of 'Mrs Leach's Fancywork Basket', price 1/6. It is the perfect antidote to that feeling of ennui after a busy day mucking out the byres and the henhouse, cleaning, baking, cooking, and so on. It would be difficult to collect between two covers a more bizarre collection of useless articles with which to waste a few hours.

A 'Hen's Head Pincushion' in brown velvet, with red comb and wattles, round beady eyes and a beak is the most grotesque, but there are lots of equally enterprising novelties. A 'Hanging Telegram Holder' in brocade and silk, for the many telegrams people no doubt received in 1902. Or why not make a cup and saucer hair combings receptacle in sateen and cardboard? Because it was a coronation year the variety of variations on this theme is endless. You could enjoy creating 'many a fancy knick-knack' such as coronation penwipers, or a paperweight using a bust of the King, a crown pincushion, or even a needle-case decorated with Queen Alexandra's favourite flower, lily of the valley, or perhaps knit a woollen purse to hold the new coins.

These patriotic works of art completed, we can start on the pingpong craze, evidently a novelty for 1902 ladies.

How about a photograph frame in thick cardboard, in the shape of a pingpong bat, with four white velvet pingpong balls stitched on? A pingpong rattle for a baby might please a sporty mother.

Perhaps 'Quaint Trifles from Marrow Bones' might fill an idle moment. 'They sell readily at Bazaars.' The bones must be cut evenly by the butcher, then after cook has boiled them for nourishing stock, or if au naturel, the nourishing contents used as a tasty snack on toast for the master of the house, boil them again till very clean, adding a pinch of washing soda to the pot. They may then be painted or gilded and turned to account in different ways. A very useful hatpin cushion may be made from one. Pass a narrow ribbon through the hollow bone, from end to end, and tie in a bow to hang. Make a roll of horsehair, cover with bright cotton, or silk, and force it into the bone which should fit tightly.

The marrow bones set upright on a triangular foundation of heavy wood or metal make curious and novel match holders for the smoking-room. If large enough, a unique flower holder is the result, which may be tinted to resemble the trunk of an old tree. These sell well at sales. I see one flaw. Where does the water go?

Now that the marrow bones are thankfully out of the way, knitting a flower pot holder would help to pass the time. You require brown crochet cotton No. 8, and two ivory or bone knitting needles No. 5, gauged by H. Walker's patent Bell gauge. The model is for a flower pot eleven inches in diameter. When complete, thread a cord through top and bottom to fit neatly. I never knew what our flower pots were lacking. Completely underdressed. People might talk.

You can study the advertisements for 'Cartwright's Middle-class Cookery', by 'Vera', price 6d, or how about 'Etiquette of Today', while knitting another useful item. How about 'An imitation feather boa, the very thing, well-suited for children's school-wear. Black ostrich and Cockatoo wools give an effect very much like that of Tibet fur, when the loops are long.' Just the thing for cold days, I might like one myself. If you have trouble with your transparent yokes, a tricky problem for delicate people who hate their woollen undervests to be visible at the shoulders, the solution is easy. Why not knit yourself a fancy opera vest, admirable for evening dresses, and a bonus – it will prevent many a chill.

There are a great many pretty patterns for pillow lace, and insertions such as rose-leaf, as well as cotton quilts, shawls, lace collars, foxglove edgings, and veils, all extremely complicated. There are knitting patterns which might be fun to try, if only to see what they are like. There are baby jackets and bonnets, dolls' clothes for the beautiful china dolls which lucky girls had, little petticoats, and boys' knee socks. The Czar visited France creating quite a craze, and at the Glasgow Exhibition Russian products featured largely. We missed that, but fortunately we can still knit the 'Mujahadin Baby Boot', a reminiscence of the top boots worn by our visitors from Eastern Europe.

As Mrs Leach advises us, 'There is often a very cosy hour or more when we like to sit chatting round the fire, between afternoon tea and late dinner. The pleasure of that hour is greatly enhanced when the hands are employed in some useful occupation.' Indeed! And after all the cook is making the dinner so no need to worry. It's fun to read about all the contrived bits and pieces but which really contribute nothing but clutter, wasted energy. Photographs from that time show so much poverty. Maybe Mrs Leach's next book gave patterns for warm shawls, and thick socks, cosy scarves and baby blankets, something to keep the bitter cold away. There certainly was a tremendous drive in the First World War for 'comforters' for the troops. And possibly a better use for marrow bones.

The swans fly in

SNOW is everywhere, drifting against the back door, piling up on the window sills. It covers the rocks down to the tide-line, fringed with wet tangle and honey ware, puckered and shiny. The sheep move slowly, munching seaweed down in the ebb, and the sea is green and sullen in the cold. Once a walrus is said to have been seen in the sea near North Ronaldsay. In this painted, glittering landscape of snow and ice, a walrus would not seem out of place.

More swans flew in last night, resting after the storms. Twenty-one whoopers slither about on the frozen loch, dove-grey cygnets try to take off, and slide ignominiously for yards on their tails. Reeds and waterweeds are imprisoned in the clutch of the ice.

These blizzards have blown up suddenly, and we are lost, cut off in a swirling, drifting, suffocating fog of fluffy snowflakes. The school has closed early today, and no lights can be seen in the smokey blue dusk. The hens and chickens have given up scratching about in the snow and have flown up into the wooden rafters of the barn roof, where they are warm, and out of the draughts from the door. They peer down sleepily from their high perch. One of the cows is over her time, and we have to keep going out to the byre to check on her. The calf is coming to a cold world.

I think snow is beautiful. Here there is no pollution at all, so the snow is pure white, and fresh and clean. The crystals are fascinating, all different, and each one perfect. The only marks are paw prints where the barn cats came to the door for their dinner. The mice are deep inside the stacks just now. Grain always scatters from the oat sheaves when the cattle are being fed, so the birds know when to fly in for extra food, blackbirds, robins and starlings. Tractors and cars make hardly any noise, and the sound of the foghorn is muffled by the falling snow.

A silent white tranquillity has settled down over the island. The shipping forecast is bad, gales and more blizzards, and in case the bad weather lasts, we have stocked up on food, but I think it will thaw before long.

Only the kittens really know how to keep warm, curled up together in a purring, furry bundle. They stoke up on extra milk, then go off to sleep, a miscellaneous bundle of paws, ears, and tails.

Frost and snow like this is better than dreich, rainy weather, when mud is a way of life. There is a snowman beside the back door, a high risk area for snowballs hurtling about. You have to be careful to avoid avalanches from the bale stacks descending suddenly from above, when you go for hay.

When the range is really hot, we can use the oven for baked apples, or baked potatoes. Hot toast and butter is good when it's snowy and dark outside, and we light all the fires to warm the air. It's Hans Andersen weather, time for reading *The Snow Queen* aloud, everyone curled up on the couch in the firelight, following Gerda on her long trek north, to find Kay in the glittering palace of ice. The golden caverns and battlements in the blazing coals make magical castles and robbers' caves, a dreamy fantasy world in the fire.

Island advent

I love advent. There is something exciting about this time, when Christmas is coming closer. Every year the days go faster, a harvest more is a harvest less, as time rushes forward, and we have to concentrate on living each day for itself. Advent with its candles and lights, its secrets and symbols, is a special time, a month of small joys in the winter darkness.

It begins with the advent wreath, made of evergreen veronica twigs, fastened to a double circle of wire, and bound with scarlet ribbons. Four red candles are fixed into the circle, and lit one after another, until all four are lit on Christmas Eve. Candles are beautiful, warm and gentle, and their wavering flames light the kitchen every night. They are the best lights for Christmas, living and vibrant, stretching back into the past, bending and sputtering as doors open and draughts swirl in from the cold night, flickering back to life, glowing yellow and clear again.

Advent is full of secrets, of presents hidden in cupboards under piles of sheets, when jerseys are waiting to be finished, and mittens and caps pile up in the wicker basket. There is never enough time, so time itself is a gift, when it is spent on making something for Christmas.

There are practical problems here in North Ronaldsay, because wool, like most other things, has to be ordered by telephone, then posted off again when it is knitted, just as everything has to be posted from our friends to us. There is no real Christmas shopping, so presents are difficult to buy and send.

It is a time for children, and for anticipation, for making cards and opening the doors and windows of the advent calendar, and for baking all sorts of things. William is good at making the Christmas cake, and he does the mixing, but everyone helps with fetching and measuring, cracking eggs, and stirring in the brandy. It is a communal effort, and all of us share the feeling of satisfaction at the lovely smell of the cake baking. Gingerbread biscuits are fun to cut out and bake, stars, men and women, all piled up on wire trays to cool. For once there are plenty of apples, so that we can bake apple tarts with a layer of home-made mince-meat.

We listen to carols on the radio, turning the dial to pick up programmes from Norway, Germany and France, as well. Carols are more evocative than anything else; they bring back the ghosts of lost Christmases, when the words made indelible pictures on the mind, and their reality was unquestioned. Even now they make me shiver with the same magic, starry skies, shepherds and angels, and frosty winter nights.

If the steamer has reached the island, we have a real tree, the only one the children see, and its aromatic scent fills the room, reminding us of distant forests far away from this treeless island. Balloons soar away into the night sky from a child's hand. Cattle chew peacefully in the byre. Christmas is still a simple festival, a sharing of hearths, when everyone is together, the room is warm, and the advent star fixed on to the light shines out through the window, golden into the dark.

Waiting for winter to die

At last the sun has come out, and is hanging low over the snowy fields and ice-covered loch. Even the sky is blue and clear, with hardly any clouds, and the wind has dropped. It has been bitterly cold for so long that last summer seems far away, in some other incarnation, as we trudge along the frozen rutted tracks. Our hands are stiff as we lift the metal snecks on the byre doors, and tug the tightly packed sheaves from the stacks.

Spring is always slow to come to the far north, and only under the sheltering dykes are there patches of fresh green grass, where small clusters of leaves of the lesser celandine are dark and glossy in the snow.

This is an in-between time for us, neither one thing nor another, and I find it difficult to settle down to do anything without feeling restless. It's too damp to paint the window frames and doors, although they need it, too dark in the evening to feel that winter is loosening its icy grip. It is the third week without a steamer. Food is monotonous, fresh vegetables difficult to get. As the days begin to lengthen so the cold begins to strengthen, and as yet another day brings iron frosts, I shiver even in the kitchen with the range turned full on.

The Cheviot ewes are heavy in lamb, although it will be some weeks before the first one is born, and the small native sheep don't begin to lamb until May, at the earliest. Calving has begun, and the calves will have a chance to grow a bit before emancipation day, when the cows are turned out at the end of April, to roll and race in the new grass, scratching themselves on the gateposts, and kicking up their hooves, before settling down again to being decent respectable bovine matrons.

Already it is pale grey dawn by seven-thirty in the morning, and every day it is light for a little longer. The birds are coming back, flocks of golden plover coming in to rest for a few days, and curlews with their long, curved beaks and plaintive call raking the fields for food. After the winter quiet, it is good to listen to the noise they make. The ground is still too hard to dig, but ploughing will soon start here, and that is the beginning of the next cycle of birth and death, the mysterious force which is still dormant, waiting for the sun to waken it from its winter sleep.

I am always filled with an indefinable sense of longing at this time, for our daughters who have left the island primary school for Kirkwall, for sunshine, for the sound of traffic, other people, houses and buildings in streets, and lights at night. The island is too silent, waiting for winter to die. I think to be truly at one with an environment such as this, which by its very nature forces the separation of parent and child, it would be necessary to be born on an island. The forces of sea and wind, the bareness of the landscape, and the wide, empty sky, need strength to endure, and this is an inborn stoicism which has been lost in urban man.

When you see how quickly a house left vacant becomes ruinous, and is taken back by grass and weather, human efforts are insignificant and temporary. Only an occasional hardy shrub, like the sweet-scented, rosy-pink escallonia, remains to show the traces of an old walled garden, and a home where once a family grew up. Perhaps it is because there are no crops growing, and the cattle are inside, that the island can be seen as it really is in itself, stripped of all human activity. There is nothing left but the bare elemental bones, the hard, rocky core, surrounded by cold seas and infinite space.

But in spring and summer, when the island comes to life again, and there is constant activity to get the crops planted, and the creel boats are going out again, then everything gets back to normal. Today is the first day this year that there has been any warmth in the sun. It is a good sign that the fields will soon dry up, and it will be hard to remember how cold it was when the loch froze over, and the moon shone on the snow through a frosty halo of ice-crystals.

The sea is not your friend

EVER. We were brought up with this truism, and so were our children. With father, brother and uncles in the Merchant Navy we knew about the sea. Living on an island it is a vital truth. When first we moved into this house at the north end, a neighbour came along to tell us about specific places on the shore which have 'sinkies', and other hazards. Only once have I forgotten, and almost paid for it with my life. This spring has been deceptively calm, but when I set off to go along the bay the equinoctial wind was rising, and there was a roar from the sea and menacing clouds building up. The 'auld wife was brewin' by the old lighthouse, breakers crashing and spume rising. There were no sheep to be seen – that should have warned me. The flood tide was high, heaps of bladder wrack and tangle washing up. But I set off as usual on my daily trip, which takes half an hour of brisk walking to our old home.

By the time I got halfway I was rapidly regretting my stupidity, but it was too late to turn back. Sandsheen, that little loch, a calm stretch of water above the shingle, had disappeared under the sea, and the banks were flooded right up to the gate. I was wading through sea water, and to reach the usual gate was impossible as the tide was pulling at my feet. I got past the old exploded mine, and managed to reach the dyke, still with waves washing up, got over the stones and on to where there was fencing wire. The sea was inland, but thanks to the wire I got to the path below the water mill, where there was more wire to grasp with both hands. It was absolutely terrifying to struggle through the two foot-high, knee-deep seawater, slungeing about and knocking me off balance.

How I ever got on to the road I have no idea. But I was never so glad to get into the warm kitchen, kettle boiling on the range, and to see my eighty-five-year-old father-in-law sitting at the table, smoking his pipe. I was treated to a well-deserved tongue lashing, the only one he ever gave me, for even attempting such a stupid venture. I was soaked to the skin in sea water, squelching boots, and dripping all over the floor. It was a salutary lesson, and a reminder that we can never trust the sea, and I would never do it again.

There are several of these old mines round the shore. Often they caused great damage and risk to life. One exploded near our house, years ago, when two of the girls from a neighbour's house were taking water from the Lady Well. That mine broke every window in our house, but the girls survived. Apparently pieces of shrapnel were scattered over a wide area. What a blast there must have been, and how terrifying.

Now the shore is almost silent, no trace of the tide which nearly got me. There is only the sound of tractors ploughing and the calling of wild ducks and gulls. We can see the Fair Isle from here, and the South Lighthouse from here. To see the island clearly, well above the horizon, rocks and crags distinct, is a sure sign of rain, but today it was faint and blurred, and the sun was bright, almost warm at noon. The birds are beginning to build their nests, and making more noise, a welcome sign.

There was driftwood all along the sea edge, after the high tide, and it always seems wasteful not to pick it up, but the further you go, the heavier the burden becomes. Armfuls of slithery damp wood are difficult to carry. There is always something more tempting further on, a length of polypropylene fishing net for stacks, a drum of deck polish, even an occasional message in a bottle. The shore seems so fresh and clean, and the seaweed glossy in the sun. The sheep have come back to graze, monitoring me with their cold and wary eyes. Early spring has its own beauty, with its wild and turbulent skies, clouds like dark wings, and Jacob's Ladders shining over the sea. Rainbows come and go as showers are blown across the skies.

Salt covers the windows, as rain carries sea spray over the island. Rust is a major problem for cars and farm machinery, and prams rust quickly in the salt air. You can taste it on your lips when you are out feeding cattle. It's good to be back in the house in the last weeks of spring while the lamps are still lit at teatime. I love lamplit evenings with drawn curtains. Soon dark winter will be over, the light growing stronger every day, and another season will begin.

Ancestral links

MARCH came in like a rather diffident lion, just trying out his strength, and prowling away again into a white sea haar. The Ring of Brodgar looked out of the fog, a vast stone circle, as we drove from Stromness to Kirkwall, on the Orkney Mainland.

The stones are at their most powerful in mist and darkness, huge and silent, as if a great concentration of power broods there. The whole area must have been an important sacred place, between two lochs. A smaller circle is close to it, and a solitary watch stone stands guarding the road.

One of the stones in the Ring is fifteen feet tall, and to see them silhouetted against the moon is a strange experience. Once there were sixty of them, but even now they are so huge that they keep their power, and concede nothing to man. Maeshowe, the finest megalithic tomb in Europe, is not far away, a large green mound surrounded by a ditch, looted by vikings who left runic graffiti on the walls. It is this proximity of past to present which gives the islands their strange timeless atmosphere.

Here in North Ronaldsay, the sea dyke forms the outer wall of an iron age broch, which was once a fortress guarding its people from an unknown enemy. Now it is peaceful, with seapinks, and soft green grass, where the floor once was, with a well in the centre. The high, skilfully built wall keeps out the wind, and you can see in every direction, for miles. On the rocks below, the sheep and sea birds take life easily. Seals turn over on the flat slabs. There is no hint of the violent past, but the broch builders have left a strange watchfulness there. Sitting on the grass, the air is full of the scent of clover, but there is a feeling that you are watching and waiting for something, a ship to come from the south, perhaps.

Even walking along the shore or in the fields, the past is close. I picked up a perfect neolithic anvil stone, probably from the mainland, because the quartz stone is unusual, and not from Orkney. It is about five inches by three, with a symmetrical indentation on each surface, where axe-heads were placed to be chipped smooth. It is comfortable to hold, and had been used recently to hammer down the stakes of chain tethers. A geologist who was staying with us found a perfect axe head in the mud of a deep ditch.

In North Ronaldsay there is a single standing stone in a field overlooking the firth. It has a hole in it, possibly connected with the position of the sun during a solstice. Cows scratch their backs against its lichened, enigmatic sides, but once the people danced around it at New Year, singing heathen songs, which were unfortunately stamped out zealously long ago. The stone must have been a major focal point, but what strange rites were enacted there, or why it stands in that particular spot is a mystery. Perhaps couples used to handfast their troth through the hole, using the ancient oath of Odin.

One of the more barbaric Norse relics is the supposed grave of Halfdan Holeg, on the links near the lighthouse. Halfdan was brutally murdered by having a blood eagle carved on his back, in revenge for killing the father of Earl Einar, in Norway.

I prefer the small, undramatic bonds, like the Norse placenames used every day, and still appropriate. The marshy path which goes from our house past the loch must have been just as mossy and damp when the Norse settlers lived here, as it is now when we take the cows and calves to their spring pasture. Its name means marshy path, and there is something reassuring in such a small detail, the name for a path just wide enough for two people to walk along together.

The wild birds and the flowers keep their old names, and just as the Norsemen left a legacy of Scandinavian words for boats and fishing, tides, sea and storm, so the women have their own continuity of living language for household tasks, children and home, cattle and food, as close a link with their ancestors as the humble house sites and the great, mysterious stones.

Time to sow

ON the island, sowing is under way, and a fresh, drying wind is blowing over the furrows, where seagulls swoop and dive, following the plough and harrows. A few people still sow the seed by hand, using the cubbie, a loop of creel wire with sacking sewn on to it, and tied round the neck or shoulders. The seed is broadcast using each hand alternately, and rhythmically, covering an area four paces in width with every handful. Black oats, an older, smaller type of grain, suited to the climate, and for feeding straight to the cattle in the sheaf, are usually sown. Only a few fields of bere, once the staple diet, are sown now.

Until mechanisation became intensive here, very little had changed over the centuries. Seaweed was gathered in the month of March, after the winter gales, using a hand barrow, a flat pallet with handles, carried by two men, one walking in front, the other behind. It was taken down to the flood mark, piled high with ware, and tipped into the cart, which was sometimes pulled by an ox. The seaweed was ploughed in, and scraped into the ground using a long-handled fork. Seaweed as a fertiliser was extremely effective, producing heavy crops.

Oxen were trained to work together, or with a cow,

from an early age. They had their own harness, including the wassie, a collar made of sacking, and filled with straw. There is a yoke for oxen in the Tankerness House Museum, which was once used in the island of Papa Westray. It is well-made, smooth with use, and has the owner's initials carved on it. Oxen were kept in the byre all winter, and well fed with plenty of sheaves, for the grain gave strength. They could plough, harrow, and scuffle turnips and potatoes, as well as pull carts. When cows were being trained to work, they began by learning to pull a piece of wood.

Horses and mares had names like Prince, Diamond, Lady, Jean, Nell, Gordon and Star. For ploughing, the trace horse led, with the rear horse between the shafts. In winter, when they were stabled, they were always walked to the lochs for water and exercise, to keep them healthy, because they got sore inflamed legs from standing for long periods doing nothing. Thrush in the hoof was another problem. There were many horseshoes under the floor of our old scullery when it was pulled down to make room for an extension. The horseman's whisper, the ancient secret bond between those who work with horses, was known here, and still may be by some of the older men.

Crops were cut by hand at first; women used the little hook, or sickle, then the scythe, but after the reaper came, two men worked together, and family and neighbours helped. Each house had its own variation of the band and knot of straw which bound the sheaf. One was the soo's tail, a twist, followed by a second twist. Another was the crook. In bad weather, sheaves which had blown away could be claimed by the owner identifying his own knot. I learned to tie sheaves with the band by watching other people, but it takes practice to do it efficiently. Now it is only needed if the binder leaves a loose sheaf.

Since everything is growing, sprouting, and taking root, I have also been making lemon curd and marmalade, opening all the doors and windows, to let in the sun, and lighting bonfires to burn the last of winter's debris.

Kill or cure

A late spring can bring feelings of malaise and tiredness. One of the tonics common to Orkney last century involved catching snails late at night, when they have a quiet feed, suspending them on a string in front of the fire, and catching the oil in a cup. Snails were used for other remedies. They were dissolved, complete with shell, in vinegar, as a treatment for rickets. Snails' heads were believed to contain a substance which reduced fever. A septic finger was tightly bound with a dressing containing a black snail, so that the poison would leave the finger.

Another cure for infected cuts, or for bruising, was fresh cow dung, which was also used for bee and wasp stings. Cobwebs were always left in byre rafters and windows, as disease preventatives, and to bring luck. Bound on a cut, the fibres, resembling the fibrin in the blood, helped it to clot.

The elder tree was used in many ways. The pith was boiled with lard to make an ointment for sprains. A lotion from its flowers cured sore eyes, and the berries were used to treat sores. The fungus known as Jew's Ear, which grows on elder trees, was thought to cure sore throats and quinsy, perhaps because of the belief that Judas Iscariot hanged himself on an elder tree.

Yellow iris, one of the commonest of wild flowers in the islands, was thought to cure stammering, if the leaves were chewed. The juice of the roots, when crushed, was inhaled to relieve toothache. Wood sage was known as gulseck grass, from the Norse for jaundice, 'gulsott'. It was infused in boiling water, and drunk. If that failed, and the jaundice persisted, the sufferer had to go to the smithy, steal a piece of rusty iron, wash it in water, and drink the resulting liquid. Only stolen iron was effective.

Earache could be cured by taking a limpet from the rocks, removing most of the flesh, and boiling up some of the liquid in the limpet shell on a red-hot coal. This was cooled, and poured into the sore car. There was no point in trying to stop an ear from discharging, because it was supposed to be the poison draining from the body. Roast mice were given to children with whooping cough. Fried herrings straight from the pan were split, and tied to the feet, to draw out the fever. I should think they would have had to tie the patient to the bed as well. The most powerful cure of all was to kill a black cat, which was placed on the stomach of a person with abdominal pain. This was a last resort cure for horses with colic.

When a horse died, or was killed, the fat was removed, and boiled up with the marrow from the leg bones. This was supposed to be valuable as a liniment for strains and sprains. People with rheumatism had the affected area thrashed with young nettles, perhaps as a counter-irritant. It was unwise to wash the feet too often, or to eat raw carrots or turnips, or to drink milk, a wise precaution in the days of bovine and human tuberculosis.

In remote islands there was no doctor, and no alternative to home remedies. Teeth were pulled out at the smithy, by the blacksmith, who had powerful arm muscles and strong pliers. Howdie wives delivered the babies and laid out the dead. It is interesting to speculate about the results of such remedies, but the hardihood of the people who could endure them is remarkable.

An invisible island

FOR days, the foghorn has been booming out, echoing and reverberating in the mist. Nothing is visible beyond the garden dyke, and I might as well be the only inhabitant, as I plant onion setts in the sandy ground. Not even our neighbour's tractor shed can be seen, and tendrils of smokey vapour drift over the blue-grey cow, as she lies chewing the cud near me.

May is a month of fog, and no other weather conditions cause so much disruption to the islands. Planes from the south are delayed or cancelled, mail is held up, and travel arrangements become chaotic, as appointments or interviews are abandoned. Children coming home for their monthly weekend wait at the airport, or circle round above the island, obliterated by dense haar. Loganair pilots can work miracles in landing the children in such weather, but it is an anxious time listening to the plane's engines, and wondering if they will have to go back to the Mainland.

I hate misty weather. The raw dampness slides under doors and windows, blotting out sunshine and warmth, while every few minutes the foghorn blasts through the fog. Sometimes these conditions can last up to three weeks, with an occasional respite, and the island is isolated in every way, both from the outside world, and within itself, as cars and tractors on the road can be heard but not seen, and no human beings are visible anywhere. The air feels heavy and oppressive, as if a great weight of moisture covers the island, chilling everything it touches. The hay in the stack is damp, and smells mouldy, and the moulting hens lurk around the shed, looking depressed.

We have entered the strange weather pattern where time ceases to have any meaning, and everything is in suspended animation. There is no rising or setting sun to be seen, and only occasionally does heat permeate the clammy, opaque milky whiteness. A few days of this, and a feeling of lethargy sinks over everything. Floors won't stay clean, because there is no fresh wind to dry them, and the ground outside grows muddy. Washing hangs inert on the lines, or dries rough and harsh over the hot range, instead of blowing outside in the sun and wind. Everything slows down, and people begin to feel depressed, in this foggy world. Accidents and sudden illness must try to wait for a more convenient time, when planes can fly. In spite of the sea just over the wall, which should bring some freshness, the air has no life or sparkle in it, and breathing is a conscious effort.

It always seems strange to see the lighthouse, the second highest in Britain, gradually vanish from sight, as fog blots out the broad white bands, one by one. Yesterday there was a ship's foghorn sounding at the same interval as the lighthouse foghorn, but not quite synchronising.

Birds come in during the foggy spells, losing their sense of direction, and resting on fences or dykes, or in the low sycamore bushes in the garden of Holland House. North Ronaldsay is on a busy migratory route, and at this time of year there are many rare and unusual birds passing across the island. Ringed pigeons often land on the roof, or the upstairs window sill, and stay until the fog has lifted. They are tame, and needing food and water, and it is always interesting to look at their ring numbers.

It is difficult to sleep through the continuous sound of the horn. Often you waken, thinking it has stopped, and the fog gone, only to hear it again at the end of a minute. There is the occasional muffled sound of a car engine, as the shifts change, and an occasional keeper goes on duty. When the fog is really bad, we listen to the late-night shipping forecast, after 'Sailing By', with more attention than usual, hoping for a change in wind direction. It takes a good blow to freshen the air, and when the grass begins to move, and the curtains lift, we know that the worst is over, and the weather will soon clear. Perhaps we could whistle up the north wind, and blow it all away.

Northern nights

THE time of day I like best is the evening, when the cattle work is done, the dishes washed, and the long, clear night enfolds us. Each small sound is intensified by the peace of the island. The blackbird with one white wing feather perches on an old malt kiln, and on the loch the ducks splash and dive, sending glittering sprays of water into the air. In the stackyard, a whole flight of butterflies dances in the sun, perching on the cow parsley, and fluttering off again.

Oyster catchers swoop overhead, the lucky bird of the Faroes, where it is called the tjelder, just as it is in North Ronaldsay. They are Saint Bride's pages, who hid the Christ-child from Herod, under seaweed, and in flight they show a white cross on a black ground. Their brilliant orange beaks are easily spotted.

All the native ewes are inside the sheep dyke in summer, and the lambs play together in the last of the sunlight, chasing each other, and trying out their horns. Our solitary orphan, a bottle-fed lamb, runs races with his shadow, leaping over hay bales and startling the mother cat with her kittens. The ducks come home with their noisy ducklings squabbling and squelching, and the chicks creep under the feathers of the hens, sensing the coming of night.

Although the island is so far north, the long light compensates for a short growing season by filling the paths and marshy places with wild flowers. Delicate pale green and white grass of Parnassus, purple orchids, enamelled marsh marigold, flourish in the damp earth. Drifts of ragged robin and bog cotton, and fragrant spires of ladies' bedstraw grow everywhere. Clumps of wild blue geranium and purple vetch grow only in one place, and near the lighthouse, bird's foot trefoil and heather cover the thin soil, where rocks elbow themselves out of the earth. Wild heartsease pansies and violets grow in the sandy ground, and everywhere the air is filled with the scent of wild white clover.

When the milking cow Peggy is brought home, her light chain tether rustles through the bright flowers of lesser bugloss and forget-me-nots. Sometimes death hides among the flowers, where the dull gold of ragwort sprouts untidily from the earth, waiting to poison cattle.

On the shore, the quiet sea whispers as it leaves a frothy line on the sand, and redshanks hurry up and down, looking for food. William and Thomas light a fire of driftwood, and the heat shimmers in the air as the sticks snap and send up showers of sparks, and resin melts in the flames. Tiny red spiders crawl over the warm rocks.

Far out, the trawlers are heading south on their way home, stretched out in the long line across the horizon. Inshore, the creel boats are fishing for cuithes. We can hear the voices of the fishermen carried on the still air.

The midnight sun hangs in the west like a golden lamp. The sky shades from crimson and apricot, through lemon, green and turquoise to deep blue. The island is suspended in a bowl of colour, and the rocks are black against the sea. Sea and sky merge together in the magical time of simmerdim. As the moon rises, the circle of the day is complete, and it is time to sleep.

The luxury of simplicity

THERE were no additives in the food eaten in the island at the turn of the century. Many families had a pig or two, and there was fresh pork to roast, fry or boil, and bones to make into porky soup, with the dark green cabbage grown in circular, walled gardens near the shore, and fertilised with seaweed every winter. Some of the pork was salted down in sweet pickle made from brown sugar and saltpetre. There was enough over to cure for bacon, which hung from the rafters. As the pigs were killed at different times, providing there was a waxing moon and a flowing tide, and since pork was used to pay debts, and given as a compliment, neighbours also got a share.

Every household had its quota of native sheep on the shore, where they lived on the mineral-rich seaweed thrown up by every tide. There was lamb and mutton, both fresh and salted, and sometimes smoked. A shoulder, or the ribs, were boiled in a big iron pot over the fire, with peas and barley, and fresh carrots and onions from the garden. Potatoes were also boiled in the pot, then the meat lifted out on to an ashet, and the soup eaten first, followed by the mutton and potatoes. Mutton was a winter food, for the sheep were at their fattest in the storms of winter, which threw tons of seaweed on to the shore.

Herring, cod and haddock, as well as saithe and ling, were caught in summer and fried in dripping, rolled in oatmeal, or boiled and eaten with melted butter and new potatoes. The surplus was dried in the sun on the stone roofs, or on lines stretched between stone walls, as in Norway. The dried fish was boiled in winter, and eaten with 'dippings' of melted butter. Salt herring was bought in small barrels of brine. In Shetland the livers of fresh fish were chopped with onion, mixed with oatmeal, and stuffed into fish heads tied with thread, before being boiled. Crabs, or partans, were also eaten.

Cows were treated well, since for one to die would have been a great financial loss. They were given extra treats, oatmeal drinks and brochan after calving, and ale, which they loved. The water they drank was lukewarm, to prevent a chill, and the milking cows were always taken in at night. The first rich milk after calving, the bees' milk, was made into a creamy cheese, which was considered a delicacy. Butter was made in the wooden plout-kirn, golden-yellow from the clover fields, to eat fresh in summer, and salted down for winter. Where possible, they tried to keep a little butter for the cold days of March, when people were weary after a long winter. Buttermilk was used as a drink, and for baking bannocks and scones, and also allowed to ferment into Bland, a fizzy drink useful in harvest-time. Any left-overs were given to the pigs.

Oatmeal, stored in the big wooden girnels, a year's supply at a time, was used for porridge, gruel, oatcakes, and brose, made quickly by pouring boiling water and a little salt on to oatmeal in a bowl, and stirring it. Mealy puddings were also made from the oatmeal, mixed with melted sheep's fat, onions, and salt, then boiled in pudding skins. If the mealy puddings were to be stored in the girnel with the meal, the onions were omitted. They could be eaten cold, in slices, or heated in the frying pan.

Bere meal too was used for bannocks, and as it was home grown and milled on the island it was economical as well as nourishing. Bere bannocks were broken into small pieces and warm milk poured over, for a small child's supper. The grop, or waste, was fed to pigs and hens. Ale was brewed from malt for harvest, weddings, yule, and when a new house or shed had to be built, there was a brewing, and neighbours worked together to put it up for no payment.

With no means of cooking or baking other than a small stove, it was wonderful that the women managed so skilfully to feed their large and hungry families, and to try to help those who had an even harder struggle to live off the land. Their diet was sound in many ways, produced almost entirely at home, and free from hormones, colourants, and preservatives, It may have been monotonous, and not to modern taste, but it must have had its advantages, for there are many people here who are in their eighties and nineties, and still fit and healthy.

The wreck of the Svecia

THE waters round North Ronaldsay ebb and flow over the wrecks of many ships. Brigs, barques and galiots lie under the cold sea. Fishing boats, emigrant ships, garrison vessels, are the graves of men, women and children, drowned before there were properly sited lighthouses, wireless, and finally radar.

The most fascinating story is that of the *Svecia*, a Swedish East India merchantman, wrecked on the reef dyke of North Ronaldsay, on 18 November 1740. There are many legends about *Svecia*'s gold, and how the sun glinted on the gold buttons and braid of the wealthy supercargoes as they floated out past the island. In that disaster, ninety-one people died.

Most of the India Company archives have been destroyed, or dispersed, and only fragments remain in Gothenburg, Stockholm and Uppsala. The State Archive and the University of Gothenburg library went to considerable trouble to help me piece together some of *Svecia*'s history. She was one of the largest and most valuable vessels of the company, carrying twenty-eight guns and with room for one hundred and twenty-eight personnel. In 1739, having returned from a voyage to Canton, with a cargo of Chinese porcelain, she set sail from Gothenburg for Bengal, under the command of Captain Rattenborg. Many Scots were among the supercargoes, Fotheringhame, Moir and Cumming, among others.

It was while they were tied up at Bankebazar in Bengal, that a Swedish guard shot down a Bengalese who was trying to break into the company factory. This gave the nabob the excuse he was waiting for to surround the factory with his men, and demand a large sum of money, in compensation for the shooting.

The crew of *Svecia* immediately took possession of the nabob's own vessel, as she lay at anchor. They also kidnapped an important official. They held the ship and crew hostage until the nabob lifted the siege on the factory, after six terrifying weeks. Eventually *Svecia* left Bengal with a cargo of silks, cottons, muslins, casks of wine, and red dye-wood lashed to the decks, to be used in textile dyes. The cargo, worth hundreds of thousands of silver dollars, was one of the most valuable cargoes ever carried by the company.

On 18 November 1740, the longest part of the journey over, *Svecia* struck the reef dyke, the hidden, underwater reef off North Ronaldsay, in a storm, and was wrecked. Ninety-one of the crew and supercargoes made a large raft, to which they attached three punts, but they were caught in the strong tidal current, capsized, and all were drowned. The ship's carpenter and twelve sailors came ashore on a piece of the ship's quarter-deck.

The Swedish consul in London was instructed to have as much of the cargo salvaged as possible. An overseer was sent to the island, and many thousands of fine handkerchiefs were washed and bleached by the women of North Ronaldsay and Sanday, and bolts of cloth and quantities of dye-wood were also saved. Some goods had been washed up on Fair Isle, and a boatload of men was sent to salvage them. Some put in claims for new shoes, because their old ones were torn out from clambering down over the rocks.

There was no proper warehousing in North Ronaldsay, and Lord Morton, the admiral in charge of Orkney waters, was asked to arrange a charter home. *Mary of Dumbarton* sailed for Gothenburg, with all that was left of *Svecia*'s crew and cargo.

While the survivors were in North Ronaldsay, they wrote to the directors of the Swedish East India Company, to complain that they had been maltreated, suffering whippings and starvation, both outward and homeward bound, under the cruel command of Captain Rattenborg, who had died during the last part of the voyage. It was never discovered exactly how he died.

In the last two years, the wreck of the *Svecia* has been located, and divers have been down several times. Cannons have been brought up, and a pair of brass dividers, a fleur de lys button, and logs still marked with the chain which secures them to the decks. Massive growths of seaweed obscure the ship, but eventually more will be recovered. It was strange to see an experiment done with wool, being turned red by the dye-wood which had been in the sea for 240 years, and which is now extinct.

Even now, when people walk along the shore after a high tide, they can sometimes find wood marked with the company insignia, a piece of dye-wood from the trees which grew long ago in Bengal, and were dragged by elephants through the jungle, on the other side of the world.

The grace of the silent swans

ALL round the house and garden dyke, the celandines are in flower, golden petals reflecting the sunshine. The grass has grown fast, bright dandelions and clumps of long-stemmed daisies are everywhere, and great bushes of sweet cicely, with their warm scent of aniseed. There are drifts of blue-bells in the garden, and growing wild in the grass.

The flag irises are growing tall all round the loch, and the winter weeds grow thick and luxuriant. Again this year two pairs of mute swans are nesting on the lochs, and visit each other almost every day. They are silent, unlike the noisy whoopers which winter with us, but they have a delicate grace, as they take off into the evening sky, or sail tranquilly across the loch.

This year the blackies seem busier and noisier than usual, singing loudly from four or five in the morning until late at night, filling the air with their exuberance. They perch on the chimneys and fly down for scraps at the back door. I seldom see the cats stalking the blackbirds, but one of them brought a live moorhen from the other side of the loch, and deposited it at my feet. After a dazed moment it recovered, and apparently unhurt, it ran away into the reeds, and swam away. Larks are high in the sky every day, sometimes almost out of sight, yet their song carries a long way. Peewits and whaups cry across the loch from the rough grass, and out on the skerry the seals are calling.

Now that the hedgehogs are awake again, we see them trotting single-mindedly along the roads and along the verges. They are always fun to watch, for they are so intent on what they are doing, and always in a hurry, as they move with surprising speed through the long grass.

Early rhubarb is growing everywhere in the old walled gardens, sweeter than the coarser tall stalks which replace them later in the year. They make better pies and crumble, and their colour is clear pink. Every spring they are a welcome change from the winter diet low in vitamins and minerals. North Ronaldsay seems to have more than its fair share of nettles. They were used by the vikings as a valuable food and medicinal plant, and there were nettle gardens as well as herb gardens round the early Norse sites. They were used both for humans and for animals, as well as in the weaving of cloth, and were used to treat coughs, stomach cramps, and to staunch blood. In North Ronaldsay, the cows used to be given cut and withered nettles, which they love, to increase their milk and cream yield.

Although I have a Swedish recipe for traditional nettle soup, I have never made it. It needs two litres of young nettles, well washed, two tablespoons of butter, and two of flour, a litre of water, two stock cubes, and chopped spring onions. The nettles are scalded in boiling water, liquidised or chopped finely, and a roux made from the butter and flour. Nettles and water, with stock cubes, and added slowly, and the soup is boiled for five minutes. Half a cup of thick cream, and some freshly ground black pepper is added just before serving. Since there are enough nettles around the dykes to fill several clothes baskets, it seems a pity not to try this recipe, and perhaps I will, before they grow too big to use.

These soft days are so peaceful, after the windy weather. In the evening we can see the planet Venus, shining clear and bright in the luminous sky.

Battling with bagels

I have just produced a batch of the world's most disastrous bagels. They are bread rolls in the shape of rings.

First of all, you make a yeast dough, enriched with eggs and corn oil, and let it prove in a warm place, until it doubles in size. Then you empty it out on to the table, roll it into round strips, and join them into rings. This is where the fun begins. Bagel dough is soft and sticky, and the rings start to disintegrate as they are being transferred from the table to flat baking tins. There were so many bagels that I ran out of tins, and had to use sheets of greaseproof paper.

The bagels grow bigger and bigger, spread out on the plate rack above the range. During this time, you are busy boiling water in a very large pan, all the while scraping off the carbonised bagel dough which has fallen on to the hotplate. There is a reason for this apparently illogical act. The bagels are going to be dropped into boiling water and cooked until they rise to the top. There is only one flaw. Bagels come to the top immediately – they don't hang about. But are they cooked or are they not?

Compromise seemed the safest solution. I took some of the bagels out of the water at once, and left the others to carry on cooking. Unfortunately, all of them collapsed while being carefully lifted out. I discarded the remains, and concentrated on the second batch. These bagels were going to stay in boiling water indefinitely, until they were presumed cooked, whether they rose to the top or not. I turned them over gingerly with a fork, so that their top sides could be boiled.

But this is not the end of the process. Boiled bagels are put on fresh sheets of greaseproof paper, and clean tins, and baked in a hot oven. The illustration showed beautiful brown and glossy bagels, obviously glazed with egg. So I brushed the boiled bagels with beaten egg, before putting them in the oven. This was not as simple as it sounds, because hot and wet boiled bagels do not take kindly to a ruthless pastry brush dipped in cold egg.

Thankfully I slammed the oven door on them, and concentrated on dropping more into boiling water. Meanwhile back at the plate rack the last batches were mushrooming by the minute, adhering to their greaseproof paper like sinister limpets. The holes in the middle had vanished, and all pretence that they were prospective bagels had gone.

A feeling of desperate urgency began to fill the kitchen. There were bagels baking in the oven, boiling in the pan, and rising on the range. The cohort in the oven were stubbornly refusing to brown. I turned the oven up to maximum and reached a crucial decision. The last batch of bagels went straight into the oven without first being boiled.

Hot and exhausted, we sat down at last, surrounded by bagels at all stages of their traumatic careers. Those which had been boiled before they were baked were heavy, pale and sad. The rebel bagels which had gone straight into the oven were light, golden and crisp. They looked every bit as good as they tasted, like portly buns.

We had them with raspberry jam and a cup of coffee, as we rested quietly in the evening coolness. We enjoyed them a lot. But I have decided never to bake bagels again.

New life

ONE of the happiest tasks for me on the island is saving life, no matter how small. The range in the kitchen has brought many creatures back, and it is the most rewarding feeling. I love saving eggs that the mother has abandoned, and carry one or two in my pocket to warm them before putting them into a small basket lined with an old towel, on top of the plate rack. You can hear them cheep inside the egg, an amazing feeling, before they start to chip at the shell and the tiny bedraggled inhabitant begins to fight its way out. They are no beauties with their oversized beaks and bedraggled feathers, but they soon dry out and can eat some oatmeal and chopped up egg. The noise they make when they want more is unbelievable. I've reared many chicks this way, and it's always a joy.

The trickiest was an egg left in a cold nest by a flighty Aylesbury. I wasn't sure how long it had been left, but the quilt of warm feathers had been disturbed when the other ducklings hatched. I thought it was a hopeless task, but worth a try, and warmed the egg gently in my pocket as usual. It took hours before there was any sign of life, but eventually the ugly duckling emerged, and gave us so much fun. She was far too small to be outside, so we made her a nest in a cardboard box. One neighbour persisted in calling her Sage'n'onion, and brought her a packet of Paxo for Christmas.

She grew very friendly, and loved to swim in the bath along with the rubber ducks, and be dried with the hairdryer. She welcomed us every morning, was friendly with the cat, and when she was bigger was able to learn to live with the rest of the brood, although it took a while to realise she was a duck and not a human. She came to the door every morning for a slice of bread. I wish I could say there was a happy ending. She had two years of the good life, splashing in puddles, eating water weeds, swimming in the loch. But there was a marauding otter going about on the prowl, killing hens, and she got not only little Sage but another three Aylesburys, and it was so sad to see the aftermath of the massacre. Otters with prey are unbelievably strong, and although I tried my hardest I could not make her let go.

We have had much happier experiences. One early morning when it was still dark and rainy I found a newborn black kitten lying on a flagstone. It was frozen and wet, and I had no thought it would live, but the range and the kitchen is always warm, and after the kitten had been wrapped in an old jumper and placed along the base of the range, I tried a drop of dilute warm milk with whisky and one squeak and it had begun to revive.

Then the strangest thing happened. Our cat Hissy came in, took one look at the kitten, grabbed it by the scruff and carried it out to her nest where she already had her half-grown kittens. I have never known a cat rear a strange kitten, although I've seen a cow rear the calf of her dead neighbour cow. The little kitten grew and thrived, fed by Hissy, and learned to be a good hunter. We called her Lucky and she is almost twelve.

We've reared many orphan lambs by the range, although the native sheep are usually very hardy. But we had a visitor who spotted what they thought was an abandoned lamb on the shore and brought it back. The mother would have been down feeding on fresh seaweed in the ebb, and would have come back calling for her lamb. We had no way of knowing which shore the lamb had come from, or we would have put it back. It was a little ram lamb, and the visitor wanted it kept inside. We had no milking cow at the time, so it was a problem. However it survived to go out eventually to the beach, when it was grown and had been bottle-fed for a few months.

We had twin calves in a big fish box from Kinlochbervie in front of the fire after a difficult calving, and although we tried everything, hot water bottles, warm blankets, colostrum, they were too weak. That was a sad morning. But the best intervention we had to make was a little calf which arrived too early to a young heifer. We took them into the byre and dried the calf with the hairdryer on the hot setting. What a wonderful sight when she began to revive and stretch, and respond to the heifer's call. And when she could stand, we named her Clairol, and the firm put her photo on their wall!

The most wonderful of all is the birth of babies on the island. As there were both doctor and midwife, it was feasible, and I have been lucky enough have had three of ours at home, although all were happy times. There were funny occasions too, when the dentist on his annual visit kindly offered to do any extractions if necessary, only an hour after the birth. But a midsummer morning with a pink sky, a cosy fire, a happy birth and a beautiful baby, what an unforgettable joy. Not every time is so perfect. Trouble can come. But if all is well, we can be grateful for one of life's most precious gifts.

Concentric circles of time

As usual, the time change has left me slightly muddled, waking every morning in the dark, at six instead of seven. I lie there wondering if it is worth getting up and making some coffee, since it is impossible to go back to sleep. The lighthouse beam, cold and white, since the old paraffin light was pensioned off and replaced by electricity, revolves every ten seconds, lighting up the room momentarily, and moving on again.

The wet autumn has left claggy fields and miniature lochs everywhere, and the potatoes are still not lifted. They are good this year, a healthy crop of Kerr's Pinks, waiting to be scrubbed and boiled in their jackets, their thin skins curling back. They are good eaten on their own, with black pepper, sea salt, and fresh butter.

The cattle are still outside, and the last of the young steers and heifers are going off to the mart, with the farrow cows. This time it is leggy Daisy's turn to go. I hate to see the old cows going away for the last time. Each has her own idiosyncrasy or eccentricity, looking round for an extra handful of cattle nuts, or giving a friendly nudge with a curly black poll. One was a compulsive muncher, grabbing a mouthful of jersey sleeve, or the back of a jacket, and licking your face enthusiastically. Molegrip was her name, because she was difficult to persuade to let go. Another was an expert at the well-timed kick with the left back hoof. Several I can remember being calved, as well as helping to calve their own offspring.

We have a young Australian research student with us, studying the native sheep. Her great-great grandfather emigrated from North Ronaldsay last century. Susan learned to spin at school, and so we are both working on some coloured fleeces. It is surprising how quickly a fleece can be spun from start to finish, but it can be painful on shoulders and finger joints if you spin all day. The brown or tanny wool is a beautiful dark colour, and there are many subtle variations in a single grey fleece, from palest smoke to charcoal often with a black stripe down the middle of the back.

Susan had been sanding down an old wheel, once used by a North Ronaldsay woman. The wheel is heavy, and made of oak, and each spoke is fixed in with wooden nails. The grain of the wool has now appeared. The treadle, footman, mother of all, base, and maidens are all made of pine, now honey coloured, with copper and brass bands shining on the maidens. There are decorative bands carved on the wheel, and it is well-made and strong. It was hard work to clean it, but now all its detail can be seen properly, and it is ready to have a new flyer put on. It is always the metal spindle which rusts and gives way, so that the flyer falls off and is lost.

I like the idea of spinning on an old wheel which has been used many times on the island. It is fascinating that Susan from Australia should be spinning the wool from the sheep she is studying, and restoring a wheel from the time of her ancestors, part of the curious continuity of the wheel of life. I often feel that time moves in concentric circles.

Winter dawn

CANDLES burn clear and bright all through the octave of Christmas and into the new year. They are almost the best part of winter, glowing steadily, warm and beautiful. Beeswax candles scent the room with the memory of summer flowers and honey. Red candles, tall and slender, burn in glass candlesticks, and white candles shine in every corner.

This winter they light the kitchen as well as the living room, saving the oil for the generator. Early in the morning their golden warmth shuts out the dark and rain. This morning the swans wakened me long before dawn, with the heavy downbeat of their great white wings, and their call, cold and remote, carried on the bitter wind. Everyone was asleep, but downstairs in the kitchen the kettles boiled on the range. The room was filled with the scent of rosin from the tree. I made some coffee, and it was warm and bright, shiny apples reflected pinpoints of flame, the copper pipes on the stove were burnished in the soft light. This is a quiet time, before the day's work has started. The cat stretches and arches her back, kneads her claws in the rug, and purrs, and the clock ticks gently.

The bread has to be started early in the morning, the yeast barming in a terracotta jug on the plate rack, and flour and salt in a big yellow bowl warming in front of the fire. The yeast froths and bubbles, and the dough rises, a fat cushion growing bigger and bigger. Plaited in three, or divided in loaf tins, with some made into wheaten rolls, it rests and proves again. Crusty and brown, sprinkled with sesame or poppy seeds, the loaves are tapped to see if they are done, and left to cool. The whole house is full of the fragrance of baking bread. This is the time to make Christmas bread, with half rye flour, and half white, mixed with melted butter, treacle, aniseed and fennel, and warm ale. The dough is made into round flat loaves, with a hole cut out with a dram glass. When they are baked, they are brushed over with coffee, and left to cool under a tea towel. Sliced thinly, and eaten with butter and cheese, this bread is delicious, my favourite bread of all, and it keeps moist and fresh.

Outside the dyke, the sheep are chewing the cud, waiting for fresh seaweed when the flood tide ebbs. They are shadows in the darkness, woolly shapes, unaware of a watcher. Overhead there is the constant drone of planes, as the men from the rigs are air-lifted home. On the shore a young seal pup has been caught in a tangled piece of fishing net, and his mother is close in, watching him. The cattle are still asleep in their warm byres, warm breath steaming up the dark windows.

The sun rises in a rosy sky. For once the rain has blown past, and the wind is fresh. Another year and another decade is nearing, with its burden of joy and sorrow, waiting on the doorstep, shaking its feathers in the cold.

In keeping with traditions

EACH tiny window in our Austrian advent calendar opens to reveal another aspect of preparing for Christmas. A grandmother sits knitting red socks beside the warm stove, a mother opens the oven door to take out a tray of biscuits. A candle is lit on the advent wreath, the tree is being decorated and parcels tied up with ribbon. A father carves a wooden toy, a child stares out into the night, children skate on the frozen canal, and sledge down the hill, birds sing in the branches of the bare trees, and in the dim blue twilight Saint Nicholas is leading a donkey loaded with sacks of toys.

These diminutive calendars are the best of all, with glimpses of warm rooms full of fascinating detail. This one has come from a friend in Vienna, who spends Christmas high in Tirol, and her letters are so descriptive you can almost smell the pine trees, and hear the crunch of snow, and the bells on the sleigh taking guests to Midnight Mass.

We also got a packet of Christollen spice, cinnamon, cloves, lemon peel, cardamom, ginger and mace, which fill the spice box with a wonderful fragrance. Four plump stollen, with butter, almonds, and fruit, with a filling of white marzipan, are cooling in the kitchen – at least there were four, but now there are three.

The scents of Christmas are instantly recognisable: newly washed curtains, rag rugs scrubbed clean and dried outside in the wind, beeswax, a drift of smoke when candles are blown out, fruit cake baking, and fresh bread. Blue hyacinths are beginning to uncurl tight buds, and there are branches of spruce, and holly, and even a bunch of everlasting flowers, all from the Borders, to decorate the rooms.

An old oil lamp burns in the kitchen, shedding its soft warm light on cups and plates, wooden bread board and a bowl of apples. A hand-turned plate made of juniper still holds the scent of the Swedish bush it came from. There is the smell of the byre, fresh hay, and the sweet breath of the cows, and their warm sleek sides, still glossy from the months in the fields. It is time to wash the blue Christmas plates which hang above the range, and tuck a sprig of holly behind each one. The tree is still in the barn, its scent of rosin and pine a foretaste of Christmas among the hay bales.

Carols fill the mind with memories of childhood. 'Snowy flakes are falling softly, Clothing all the world in white. Far above, the stars are shining, Twinkling through the wintry night', almost forgotten and seldom heard, but beautiful in the simplicity of its Polish melody. I am listening to Hely-Hutchinson's Carol Symphony, which has always given me a great deal of pleasure, and I always listen to it during advent. It is the very first Christmas music I can remember, an evocation of magic which never fails, the wonderful music for 'The Box of Delights' on *Children's Hour* on the wireless.

Behind the thick warm curtains the glass of the window was cold. Outside the planets were spinning away in the icy darkness of space. There was a secret world outside, a mysterious blue dusk, where snow was falling silently covering the streets and gardens, a world of bells and snow crystals, stars and moonlight. Shepherds were out on the hills, angels hovered near the earth, their great wings shining in the light from the star, their voices high and clear and cold, like icicles. The Three Kings were journeying through the desert, swaying on their camels, bringing their gifts, foreshadowing death as well as birth.

Inside the room the fire was burning red and the lights from the Christmas tree glowed golden and rose-pink, silver and blue. My mother was wrapping presents, cards were being written, and stockings were ready to hang on the brass rod above the kitchen stove. Everything was warm, and familiar and secure. But the strange and beautiful music wrapped me in its spell, drifting out into the snowy dusk and up into the shining stars.

Startomatics

ONCE again we are living in a blue twilight island of snow and ice. We waken in freezing darkness, breath smoking in the air, to a cold world. Icicles hang from the roofs of barn and byre, long, glittering stalactites, which the children break off and put in their lemonade. We cooled a bottle of wine in a snowdrift, and set a trifle in a pail of snow.

The rutted road is deep in snow, and frozen slush has iced over, making it dangerous to walk on. Snow crunches under our feet, as we lift the net back from the big bale stack, and go into the sweet-smelling hay to pull out bales for the cattle. Sometimes a furry paw, claws extended, pounces on to an unwary hand, when one of the cats suddenly wakes up inside the stack and thinks he hears a mouse. We warm our cold hands on the backs of the Herefords as they chew hay and sheaves of oats. The year-olds are friendly and curious, always licking and nuzzling whenever they are fed.

The nights have been still and clear, the frosty sky sparkles, and the merry dancers glow in the north, pale and green. With a generator for electricity, the lights in every room are switched on, to provide enough pull for the engine, a puzzle for visitors, who are used to switching off every unnecessary light. There are outside lights fixed high up on the roof of the old croft house, which was the home of the former occupants until they built the present house in the twenties. The old walls are thick, and hardly a sound can be heard from the startomatic, as it chugs in the night. If you walk across the grass near the old house, you can feel the kilowatts vibrating under your feet.

Years of washing nappies and clothes without hot water and electricity have made me appreciate the generator. It means that we can have a washing machine and spin dryer, but not an electric kettle, which needs too big a surge of electricity. We can use a vacuum cleaner, but not at the same time as the washing machine. A heater would also be too heavy, and would overload. But television and a tape recorder are a blessing, especially in the long darkness of winter. Children get their first and often distorted view of the outside world from television, and become aware of the contrast in environment more easily, when they can see the hills and forests of the mainland, as remote in appearance as another planet, to their treeless, windswept island.

Occasionally the generator breaks down, and we are back to the oil lamp, the Tilley, or candles. It is always a relief when there is a crackle on the radio, signalling that the lights are coming back on. It is frustrating when right in the middle of a good television thriller, the picture suddenly begins to get smaller and smaller, and there is a rush to switch off before any damage. The worst break down we have had occurred when the engine suddenly went off, and we found that the big fly-wheel had come right off the generator. Fortunately it landed on the floor, but it could have gone right through the wall.

A powerful engine is a good defence against elemental darkness and storms. Sometimes I can start the generator myself, after it has refused to come to life, by squirting a quick-start spray. We have to be extra careful about saving oil in winter, in case of running short in stormy weather when the steamer can't reach us, so we wait until it is completely dark before switching on, and only having it on for an hour in the morning, to do the cattle work.

Now the afternoon is closing in, and dry, fluffy snowflakes have started to drift down over the dykes and roofs. It's time to go outside and feed the cows. I have been heating mittens and woolly socks inside the range. It wouldn't be the first time I have discovered a heap of ashes in the oven, but the glorious feeling of warm hands and feet make the risk worth while in this snowy January.

Time and tide

Autumn's cold winds are blustering across the island, but Saturday was mild, and we went to the shore for a walk. We climbed over the stile built into the dyke, two heavy flat stones projecting four feet and two feet above the beach. Generations of sheep have worn a path along the hard-packed sand under the shelter of the wall, and below it are the rocks and boulders thrown up by the sea.

The tide had gone out, so we could go right down to the edge of the translucent water. The sand here is coarser than on the east and south side of the island, and is good grit for the hens. The water scarcely moved, languorously easing its way out of the bay, leaving frothy bubbles. All the seals had gone out with the tide, to lie on Seal Skerry, and hardly a bird was hunting among the fresh seaweed.

Only the sheep, eating the ware, kept lifting their heads and watching us speculatively with their yellow eyes. They move ahead of us without haste, then, as they reach the boundary of their territory of shore, they turn and run back past us. They inherit this ancient knowledge, and no matter which beach the ewes are returned to after lambing, they unerringly and quickly find their way back to their own part of the shore.

We were looking for a message in a bottle, but in the calm weather very little had been thrown in by the tide. The boys were having a trial of strength, to see who could throw the biggest stone into the deepest rockpool to make the best splash. The sun sparkling on the water, even in haze, fills children with joyful excitement. They jump up and down, shriek with delight at the leaping water, and are close to the reality of beauty which lies at the heart of all life.

It is the wetness and saltiness of the water, as it stings their skin, and the gritty texture of the damp sand as they squeeze it in their fingers, that they experience with an intensity poignant in its transcience. They laugh and chase each other with long wet tangle stalks, clawed at the ends with gnarled brown roots, then suddenly discard them and throw them into the sea.

Best of all, they love to find bladderwrack to pop with their thumbnails. Shells too appeal to them, broken and whole, narrow strips of pearly limpet, tiny bright yellow winkles, and opaque green fragments of glass, their jagged edges buffed into subjection of years of pounding in the surf.

They pick up handfuls of wet green weed which covers the rocks at low tide, squeezing it out like a sponge. They like to write their names on the sand or draw pictures, sometimes even a continent with islands and settlements. There is something spacious about drawing on such a large canvas. Absorbed in the bright bubble of the present, the boys are unaware of the passage of time. The facility to live totally in the present moment seems to belong only to children.

Harvest moon

THE full harvest moon rises low and golden in the sky, lighting the fields of stooks with unearthly beauty. There is always a quietness about the last few days of autumn, when the wild geese are resting on the stubble, gathering strength for the journey south. Soon the swans will come back from Norway, flying in graceful conformation, to land on the loch with a scarcely perceptible ripple. It is part of the recurring pattern of life on the island that they should see and recognise the loch, as they fly across the dark and starry sky.

The cattle are still out, grazing the last sweet grass. Mushrooms as big as saucers, and small round puffballs appear by magic overnight, to be gathered and cooked gently in a little butter on the range.

This year the harvest is late, with the oats having to be cut while they were still green. There was too little sun to ripen them, and then the gales and rain ravelled and tangled the crop, making cutting long and difficult. There are still some fields waiting to be cut, but most of it is stooked. The ley oats were long and heavy, and these sheaves are always difficult to handle. They had to be pulled apart before stooking, and it was hard to find good sheaves of equal size and length. Many were loose and had to be bound by hand. Instead of the usual dry grain, easy to handle, and firm earth, everything was wet and muddy. All the stooks had eventually to be moved over, to give them a better chance of drying out.

It is a strange experience to be stooking a field of oats with the children, the whole family working together to get the harvest in, and seeing gigantic oil rigs being towed past the island on the way to the oil fields in the North Sea. Overhead there is the drone of planes and helicopters coming and going to Shetland. Yet the old familiar harvest work goes on, echoing other centuries and past generations, links in the endless chain which binds man to the earth in both drudgery and elation.

Pitching the heavy sheaves on to the trailer is hard work, and there is an art in pitching accurately, and building a good load, with a strong centre. It's easier building the load, and then there is the ride back to the stackyard, and since the fields are scattered, it is quite a long trip, swaying high above the road, holding on to the ropes. The sheaves smell so good, malty and wholesome, and the clouds scud along in the light blue sky.

A slow, careful turn through the gate, and into the yard, and then there is a quick descent from the load on to the grass. Then comes pitching the sheaves on to the stack, after a hasty cup of coffee or tea. This is harder than pitching on to the trailer, as the stack gets higher. I hate pitching sheaves from the top of a load on to the top of a high stack. It makes me dizzy.

This year we found only one mouse under a stook. Sometimes there are many, and once we saw a field mouse moving slowly along with seven young ones clinging to her long tail. Perhaps it was too wet and cold for many to survive. In several fields, migrating flocks of birds stripped the oats entirely from the straw. Usually the crops are in the yard before the migration is in full spate.

Now at least the harvest is over, and it is time for the cattle to come in to their warm byres out of the cold and rain. But we may still have some late sunshine before the potatoes are ready to lift, and we let this autumn, like all the others, stormy or still, go drifting over the receding horizon into the past.

The scent of night

THE immensity of the starry dark always makes me shiver, when I peer round the sheltering gable at the sky. We took four of the cattle home from a field a mile away, in the bright moonlight. The heifers were quiet and steady, and the blue-grey cow led, her neat hooves clicking on the road. Their clean, sweet breath smoked into the sharp night air, and the sea was pewter, caught in the grip of frost.

Everything smelt fresh and cold, a mixture of seaweed and the Atlantic, late grass and drifting smoke. It was exhilarating to be out on such a starry night, listening to all the sounds of darkness, the throb of generators, dogs barking as they heard us pass, other cattle coming up to fences to watch, snipe and curlews calling. The island is never quiet at night, always there are birds or seals, a car in the distance, wild geese flying over. The cow I was leading was going to the mart, plodding peaceably along the familiar road for the last time.

In the yard in the moonlight there was more livestock, a baby hedgehog snuffling and rooting around in the grass. He rolled up into a tight ball when the cats came up for a quick look, and snorted and grunted at them from inside his prickles. He seemed to be quite unafraid of us, and we could see the light brown of his face, and bright black eyes, and surprisingly long legs, as he dug holes in the earth, all the time making a great deal of noise for something so small. We have seen him several times since then, rooting about, and squeaking bossily, so perhaps he has decided to stay and hibernate.

The sky begins to darken imperceptibly about three in the afternoon, then very quickly the night rolls in, blotting out the rest of the island. Only the house lights of crofts can be seen, and their outside lights shining from the tops of barns and byres. It is easier to pull the sheaves out of the stack before it gets dark. They are tightly wedged in, and it takes a hard wrench, gripping the twine round the middle before they come out with a jerk. Each animal gets a whole sheaf, and the cats stalk around waiting to pounce into the space left by the sheaves.

People have to be careful this autumn, to protect themselves from farmer's lung, easily contracted from mouldy hay. The wet summer has left this year's crop in poor condition. Before we had the baler, we twisted 'windlins' of hay for the cattle, winding a bundle round the arm, and twisting in the end. It takes a hot, dry summer to dry the scented hay. The fragrance lingers in the stacks all winter, bringing back sunny August with the sudden drift of clover and meadow grass.

The scent is so evocative that I am back in childhood, feeling the dry, prickly hay on my bare ankles, helping to rake, and eating bread and raspberry jam in the shade of the ricks. Sometimes it is our own children that I see, tucked up in the pram in the field, or running between the coles, sliding, bouncing in the soft, new hay, scratched by withered brown thistles. Like beads on a silver chain, the seasons roll past, called back for a second by the sweet scent of the hay.

November lamplight

FIRELIGHT keeps out the dark and cold of the winter night, as we draw the thick curtains against the blue dusk. This is the time for making the puddings, jewelled with cherries, silver charms, slivers of almonds, and fruit from sunny countries. Wishes and brandy are stirred up together with a wooden spoon, in the big yellow baking bowl. Cinnamon, nutmeg, mace and ginger spice the air. Poems and pictures on the kitchen wall, blue Christmas plates, lustre jugs, take on a new aspect in the soft light. Tall shadows hide in dark corners, leap out, and vanish again.

Waves of heat shimmer up from the hotplate, and the kettles sing. Socks and shoes and clogs are drying, and firelight enfolds us. Dreams and memories tick over with the clock, and old songs tug at the mind, kindled by the fire, for November is full of ghosts. Souls and saints, candle-bearers in the dark night of the past, pause for a moment as the year nears its end, then drift away again into forgetfulness.

There are apples baking in the oven, packed with raisins and butter, for it is a shame to waste the heat. The wooden walls are permeated with the faint scent of rosin, and oil lamps and smoke.

We seldom use oil lamps now, except at bedtime, unless there is a generator failure, but their light is warm and friendly. I don't like cleaning and polishing the lamp glass, because it is so fragile, and the chimney is very narrow. It is rubbed with methylated spirits to remove the soot, washed in warm, soapy water, dried carefully, then polished with a clean rag. Oil is poured into the base, a tricky job requiring a steady hand to prevent an overflow, and the wick is kept trimmed. It is easy to control by turning up or down. If the flame is turned too high it changes from clear to orange, and begins to smoke and blacken the glass. But at the right height, it gives a beautiful light, warm, and comforting, and peaceful.

It is a perfect light to read in bed by, illuminating the pages with its steady glow, and leaving the rest of the room in shadow. Its warmth induces sleep, and when it is turned down to a faint blue star, and blown out, a faint spiral of smoke lingers in the night. I shiver in spite of the warm quilt, for outside are the whirling constellations, and the island is a dark rock between sea and starry sky.

The icy light of the winter moon sometimes wakens me, and I stand at the window to watch the water of the loch reflect its path. The swans are restless in the moonlight, and suddenly take off, calling to each other as they rise above the fields and fly towards the north. I hear the beat of their wings as they cross the bay, dark shapes against the spinning stars, then come in with hardly a splash. Their vibrant wheeling grace is the only movement in the sky, and no lights can be seen anywhere. Bare toes on the cold wooden floor chase away swans and stars, and send me back to bed.

Winter's darkness is brightened by lamplight and starlight, and there are only a few short weeks until the shortest day, and the gradual strengthening of the daylight as the spring sun comes nearer.

A time to spin

We have had someone staying with us for a fortnight, who wanted to learn to spin, so the spinning wheels came into the kitchen again, along with the lazy Kate, and the reel, and a sack of fleece, as well as a pile of newspapers to tease the wool on.

You need room to collect everything together, space to spread the fleece out on the floor to sort it, and to tease it out. Then it has to be carded into rolags, which are light and so free from tangles that you can see through them when you hold them up to the light. The carders are flat wooden boards with nailed pads of sharp steel teeth. Carding is an art which is not easy to learn, and good spinning depends on skilled carding. The wool is combed out with the top carder, held in the right hand, then the action is reversed, so that the wool is turned over. When the fibres are pulled out and clear, the rolags, or rowers, are rolled off very lightly. Twelve rowers make a kneuk, and then we can begin to spin. You can keep the carded rolags in a wicker basket close to your hand, to ensure the continuous and even movement of the wool on to the bobbin. I usually put them over the metal bar of the range, because the warmth makes them fluff up, and spin easily.

The rolag is held in the left hand, and fed into the wheel with the right, while the wheel is treadled. The wool is held on a series of hooks on the flyer, and wound on to the bobbin. As the wheel goes round, and the wool is pulled in, the twist enters the rolag. The wheel makes a gentle whirring sound, and the treadle a rhythmic thud, and the synchronised movements of hands and feet are beautiful to watch.

When the bobbin is full of wool, it is removed from the spindle, and put on the lazy Kate or Sweerie, and another bobbin filled. Two bobbins or three are then plied together on an empty bobbin, by reversing the wheel and spinning backwards. Then the plied wool is wound in a figure of eight action on a wooden reel, a rod with a bar at each end at right angles to each other. This hand-made reel from the last century is made to a specific length, so that the wool could be wound in hanks of known length, threads counted, and quantities calculated. The vikings used a similar device, without the right-angling of one bar. The hanks are tied firmly in at least two places, and scoured in hot soapy water twice, then rinsed and dried outside. It is smooth in texture, fine, and very soft.

It's best to spin the wool as soon as it is carded, rather than to card a basketful, and leave it overnight, as the rolags are never so light and full of air on the following day. So it is necessary to be able to concentrate solely on spinning for a few hours at a time.

Spun wool seems to be much warmer than commercially produced wool, and it has been well worth learning to spin, to use some of the coloured fleeces, in every shade from cream through brown and grey to black. It is ideal here for keeping out the rain and cold, for mittens for outside work, because it is so hard-wearing and warm. It is also perfect for children's socks, for feet that are chilled in rubber boots. Care has to be taken to adapt a knitting pattern to suit the wool, and even a tension square isn't a sure guide, for the result is always larger than intended, possibly because of the air trapped in spinning.

It is especially interesting to knit two- or three-colour patterns; not only are they warmer, but Swedish, or Norwegian patterns look good knitted in North Ronaldsay wool. It is very easy to be bewitched by spinning, after a lapse of a few months, and to spend every spare moment producing hanks of soft, warm wool, but it can give you sore shoulders, and painful fingers if you persist too long. To transform raw, unprepossessing fleece into beautiful hanks in subtle shades, or white wool which can be dyed with madder to produce apricot and russet, or with lichen, or many other plants, is an exciting and rewarding activity, and the product is so useful that we never have enough spun wool.

Spring sunshine

SCARLET geraniums bloom horizontally in the kitchen window, following the low winter sun across the sky. All through the dark weeks, pink and red clusters of blossoms have brightened the window sills, flourishing in spite of neglect. With joyful Mediterranean abandonment, they tumble out of the hanging flower pots, and twine their ivy leaves tenderly together.

Not a single frail snowdrop spike or a bold daffodil has poked up through the wintery ground, and no celandines have appeared below the dykes. The year William was born on the island, his birth was welcomed with the sweet, sharp scent, and delicate green scalloped edging of a bunch of snowdrops from the garden, but this year, spring is late.

The grass is still brown and leached, with no sign yet of fresh new growth, even in the marshy land around the loch, where the water weeds are drab and pale. On the shore there are none of the brilliant ambers and greens and corals of summer. The seaweed is sparse, and only tangles with their long stalks, and bladder-wrack lie on the tideline, where the sheep are nibbling desultorily.

During the holidays the boys were down at the beach gathering tangles, and the bundles are drying in the old shed at the sea dyke, once used for drying cow dung for fuel. The stone walls are not mortared, to allow gales to blow unhindered through them, and it serves a useful purpose drying tangles and storing driftwood. If the bundles had been left on the stone steethes built for the purpose on the shore, they would have been washed away by the high spring tides, when the sea comes right through the dyke, knocking it down.

We haven't been along the shore to see if the otters' tunnel in the bank is still there, or if falls of sand and storms have blocked it up. When it is clear, the otters can go from the loch to the sea, under the grassy bank. Sometimes down at the edge of the water you can see them, on a dark night. Tommy saw a family of otters, sleek mother and several young ones, playing in the clear water beside an old pier, but they are a rare sight here. They are said to give a savage bite if cornered, and are treated with caution.

The whooper swans have been spending their days at the back of the byre. They are undisturbed by anyone taking bales from the stack, and merely call to each other, and stretch their great wings, when they see us coming. Three cygnets from last year, and their parents, they are big, heavy birds, plodding through the winter grass, and rooting in the marshy places. I shall miss them when they fly north again for the summer. The heron too, with his gawky long legs, stalks close to the edge of the loch.

Already the calves have started to arrive, although most of them will not be born until summer, when the cows are outside on the grass. There is a much greater variety of breeds now, Aberdeen-Angus, Hereford and Charolais,

Jersey, Ayrshire, Friesian, Cumberland Shorthorn, and the old-fashioned blue-greys, a good milking strain. So far no lambs have been born.

Every day the light grows stronger, and soon we will be able to leave the generator off until five in the evening. In a few weeks we will be able to plant some morning glory seeds in two inch pots in the linen cupboard, so that we can have an early display of flowers round the windows, climbing quickly to unfurl their striped sky-blue trumpets in the sun.

Noisy nights

YOU would think that it would be quiet here on the island at night, that there would be no sound but the lap of waves on the rocks. On the contrary, it is so noisy that if we forget to close the window that faces out to sea, at the top of the stairs, someone has to get up later to shut it. Every night, as soon as it is dark, the seals begin their choir practice.

It starts fairly tentatively, just a faint, petulant query from a female, answered by a growl, then all the rest join in the discussion. Howls, snorts, wheezes and grunts reverberate in the water just over the dyke, and within minutes the choral society is in full voice. Waves of querulous sopranos echo round the bay, answered by the mellow tenors, with a few deep bass bellows thrown in as make-weight. They sound like dogs, or wolves, howling in harmony, and the noise has to be heard to be believed.

If it is foggy, the din is even louder. Seals seem to enjoy singing in the fog, or perhaps sound acts as a kind of direction finder for them, for the air is full of their howls. Since autumn fog lasts for several weeks, choir practice continues unabated every night, with full scale performances at high tide. The fog horn, with its eight trumpets booming simultaneously every two or three minutes, blasts through the mist. In its wake, the seals join in, presumably admiring its resonance and volume, perhaps even contemplating whether this might not be the Great Seal itself giving voice.

When the tide is at full flood, there are often well over two hundred seals in the bay, just below the house. They are safe from any hunting, and unafraid. The sound of a human voice attracts them, and they come up to listen. Music from an accordion, or the radio, brings them in close.

The night is full of voices. Birds start up suddenly, and fly out of the reeds round the loch, crying to each other.

Snipe drum nervously, and startled peewits call out, but this year we have heard no corncrakes, perhaps because there are no crops round the house. Far off a dog barks at a sudden sound, a car goes past on the way to the lighthouse, and there is the hum of a plane overhead. Out at sea, ships' engines hum, warned off by the foghorn.

Even on a calm night, the sea roars as it strikes the rocks at the west beach, and when I came here first I used to wake in the night thinking I was back home. The sea sounds very like distant traffic. Up near the coastguard hut, where the rabbits have their warrens, there is an occasional sharp cry, as a cat pounces on a young one. The cats who live up there and hunt for all their food, come home only rarely for a bowl of milk, and some company. They purr, and weave round ankles, then disappear again, chased away by the mother cats, who snarl and spit at them, protecting their kittens from strange marauders.

The only cure for those noisy nights is to get up, go downstairs, shake the sleepy kettle on the range, to make it sing, and have some hot cocoa in a pink flowery mug. The kitchen is at the front of the house, and much quieter than the bedroom. I can tuck my feet up under a rug, read some good escapist fiction by candlelight, and seals, fog, and darkness vanish away.

The keeping of the wells

THE grey skies of autumn are banking up in the north-east, and wind and rain drives away the sun. Summer seems to vanish faster every year. For a few weeks, the delicate veined scarlet poppies blew among the growing oats, wild violets and speedwell grew in the sandy soil, and a pink haze of ragged robin and rosy red orchids covered the lochside. The scent of clover was everywhere, and golden flag irises followed the marsh marigolds. In spite of so many flowers, we have seen no butterflies or bumble bees at all this year, and not even a wasp has come looking for jam.

Some of our cows are half a mile from the house, and in the morning and evening we followed the old grassy path which leads past the loch with its ducks and moorhens, listening to the screaming gulls and anxious oyster catchers. Two white pigeons with rings live in a ruined croft, calm and unconcerned at the approach of feet.

There is a small well in the cows' field, covered by flagstones, with narrow steps down to the water. It isn't deep, and every morning the water level has risen just enough to fill the drinking trough, although the water table is low at this time of year. Springs and wells are fascinating. It isn't surprising that legends and proverbs surround them, and that they have names like Lady Well. Sometimes they are named after the men who made them, or the people who used them.

This little well with its sandy sediment and clean water smells fresh. There is no green slime on the stone sides, and once a rabbit shot under my hand as I lifted the flagstone over it. The cows come and stand beside us while we fill their tank, trying to chew jackets or lick ears. I can sit on the edge to fill the pail without having to go down the steps.

We have a much deeper well just across from the house, which had to have buckets lowered down many feet on a rope or chain, to the water. During very dry spells, we have taken water for cattle, and for washing clothes from it. I don't like wells with slippery steps, and echoing dark depths.

I wonder how all those water sources were first found. All the wells are very old, and are marked on the old charts. It must have been especially hard on the women to draw water for all the household's needs, and for the cows. There would have been no waste, when every drop had to be heaved up from the murky innards, and carried for a considerable distance over rough ground. A good well near the house must have been a great help, where there were large families of children, or the people were old. Not all of the wells could have been clean, and a level of contamination must have been present in all of them.

Keeping wells properly covered with heavy flagstones which have to be dragged off and replaced every time they are used is hard work. The stones have to be too large and heavy for children or cattle to be able to dislodge them, and they have to be replaced to make a stable surface, completely covering the well.

No children seem to have fallen down a well here, but very rarely there have been cattle. When our children were small, we filled in our other well at the side of the road, with trailer loads of stones, because it was too accessible, and too tempting to play beside, or to drop pebbles in to hear the splash, but at one time it must have been very useful to have a well near the house, and on the road.

Soon the cows will be back home. The hay is baled, and the shearing is over As the population gets smaller, those on holiday from school or university help with the work. This year for the first time we have no cereal crop. There will be no fields of stooks rustling in the sun and wind, no pitching sheaves on to trailers and stacks. The tarry smell of binder twine, blistered fingers and scratched ankles have gone for ever. Never again will the old binder break down in the tangled crop. Often October was almost over before the harvest was done, but the word carries images of golden grain, with all the symbols and significance of corn and bread, and life itself. Hay bales have none of the beauty of sheaves of barley and oats, but they are quicker and easier to produce. Even in North Ronaldsay time is moving, and not only the seasons are passing.

Harvest home

NORTH RONALDSAY always has a late harvest home, waiting until the weekend in November when the children come home from school on the Mainland. The old wooden hut, built for servicemen returning from the First World War, has been superseded by a new community centre. The old atmosphere has been kept by decorating the walls with sheaves, sprayed out to make golden circles of grain. There are twisted ropes of straw, called simmons, knotted at intervals with bunches of coloured cork floats. Lighted candles are fixed into holders, with veronica twigs. The corn and oats smell malty, and transform the hall into something different and more mysterious. The harvest home is the focal point of the island year, the time when all the hard work of ploughing and sowing has resulted in a good crop, or a wet, ravelled tangle of grain.

By the time the harvest home comes along. I have forgotten about the harvest, for the bright blue autumn days have blown away with the October gales, and the bales are stacked long ago. Winter is here, with its dark, starry skies, and snow and hail batter on the roof of the centre as we eat our harvest supper. We used to have a last minute dash to collect six forks, knives and spoons, before going to the old hut, but the new centre has crockery and cutlery. The supper used to be mutton and clapshot – turnips mashed with potatoes – and now it is cooked ham and pineapple, with clapshot.

After the meal, there is a toast in cider to the harvest, and to the island's future, people are elected to the community association, and then the tables are pulled back, and the accordions brought on to the platform. There is a great difference between live and recorded music for dancing. The hard-working accordionists give so much life to the evening. Their staying power is remarkable, supporting heavy, full size accordions hour after hour in the heat, and playing fast reels and slow waltzes. The music and dances change very little with the years, although at one time the Palais Glide and Eva three-step must have been new-fangled. The Strip-the-willow danced here is not at all the same as the traditional one, but much more fun. Small children love the dances, and are either carried on one arm, or whirled round the floor by an adult, if they are big enough. When they are tired of dancing, or chasing each other round the hall, they climb up on someone's lap for a quick rest. They always enjoy sliding up and down the floor, especially when there is a cup of tea halfway through the evening.

It is a good time to see how all the children have grown, and who they resemble, and how the babies have come on since the last meeting. A gathering like this, where everyone is known to one another, is rare now, except in such small places, and it is one of the strengths of the community. It re-establishes the sense of belonging to a group, and there is always a strong family feeling. There is a different atmosphere at this meeting to any other through the year. Perhaps it is because the harvest work is over, and there is a feeling of relief that the crops are in, in spite of everything, and the creel boats ashore for the winter.

Long ago, this shared sense of achievement must have been even greater, when the work of harvesting was shared, and there are old photographs of reaping, and leading home, which show how many neighbours were involved in getting the crops in. Since much of the island's food for both people and animals depends on a good harvest, the thankfulness when it was safely over for another year must have been much greater.

Now that the harvest home is over, and the cattle beginning to be brought in, and huts tied and wired down in case of gale damage, we are well into winter, an end and a beginning in the unending cycle.

Under the snow

LIKE an engraving etched on glass, the frozen reeds are imprisoned in ice, and the swans sleep, heads tucked under wings. Their feathers seem pure white, yet against the snow they are a warmer, creamy colour. The loch has frozen over, and the whole island is under more than a foot of snow.

We had to bring two heifers home from another croft, very late at night, because the forecast was so bad that it would have been difficult to reach them later on. We set off about ten in the evening, along the short cut by the loch, through deep snow, and the full moon was swinging high above us, casting black shadows on the drifts. It was as clear and bright as day, and we could see the whole island sparkling white, and all the stars glittering above us.

I had to walk like the page, in Tommy's footsteps, for it became exhausting to lift my feet out of the snow to take a step, and because of the depth, the path was obliterated, so that we tripped in hidden ruts. It seemed a long two miles, yet the unmarked snow was beautiful. Near the burrows, beneath the deserted coastguard hut, there were rabbits' paw prints cut deep where they had come out for food.

All the time we had to watch the sky for clouds, for if blizzards had come, we could have got lost, and wandered into the loch, but it was hard to hurry through the snow. The cattle were sheltering in the lee of the dyke, and came to us at once, although they had never been on tethers. They plodded through the white fields to the path, and above us the whole sky suddenly lit up with an amazing display of the aurora borealis. Due north, there was a blood-red column of clear light, rising out of the sea, an eerie and awesome sight, massive in size and reaching up into the very depths of the sky. In the north-west, yellow streamers began to sway like gigantic curtains, and a diffuse green glow built up on the northern horizon. Below this celestial display two ships, all lit up, sailed past us to round the point where the lighthouse stands.

Still the cattle plodded on through the drifts, as though they knew where they were going, and the dark snow clouds banked up behind us every minute; whenever a cloud blew across the moon, the night seemed far darker and more threatening. We got them safely past the loch and the sleeping swans, and into the yard and shelter, with hay from the stack, and fresh water. The other cattle began to bellow and make a fuss about the new arrivals, turning round in their stalls to stare and stamp. One of the heifers planted a neatly aimed hoof at my knee, which seemed a poor reward for the night's work. It was a relief to get into the warm house, take off boots and oilskins, and have a midnight supper in front of the fire.

Snowy nights bring one glorious luxury, a bedroom fire. It's too cold to sleep upstairs when the temperature is so low, so every night the fire is lit downstairs. I love watching the shadows on the walls and the golden flames in the grate. There are pictures in the red heart of the fire, and the crackle is cheerful and friendly, when the wind is howling outside and rattling the doors.

Creepies for comfort

EVERY house in North Ronaldsay has an indispensable piece of furniture, the wooden creepie, or milking stool. Simply made, sometimes from driftwood, or from good pine, they are versatile and attractive. They have a hole in the top for picking them up, either heart-shaped or round, and they are very comfortable seats. All creepies are solid, and down-to-earth, with no frivolity in their construction, and most are low, only about a foot high.

There are miniature creepies, only six or eight inches off the ground, for small children, and they are ideal for sitting in front of the television, or for having supper at the fire. Children often sit on the floor and use their creepies as small tables to draw or write on, or to hold a plate and mug. Bigger creepies are used for all kinds of games. Turned upside down, they are dolls' cots or teddies' prams, sledges, boats, trains and cars. With their smooth, flat tops they can be pulled along, outside or in, and they are so low that they never tip up, ejecting their passenger on to the grass.

They are ideal for sitting down to bath a baby in front of the fire. Their low height is perfect for lifting a baby in and out of the water, and drying him or her on the lap, and also for feeding. They are useful as extra seats, and a basket of knitting or sewing can be kept on a creepie beside an arm chair. They fit into a small space, and hold half-written letters, newspapers and books. We are using an old scrubbed creepie to hold eight or ten small houseplants, because the window sills are full.

Outside, there is usually a creepie for milking, either one which is no longer used in the house, or a heavier, cruder stool. In summer, a creepie can be taken out into the garden, and you can dry your hair in the sun, or have a cup of coffee in the morning.

These stools must go back far into time, because of their simple construction. No lathe is needed, because the legs are two planks of wood, not turned, as in three-legged stools. Young boys and girls learning woodwork make creepies. We have a tiny one, only three inches high as a piggy bank.

The stools have a sadder use. When someone dies, the coffin rests on two creepies during the service in the house. These are often just the ordinary household creepies, but there are special ones for the purpose, used in the church. There is something dignified and appropriate in using such familiar wooden stools. It used to be the custom in the north-east for these creepies to be knocked over after they had been used, to prevent them being used soon again. Nor were they ever left in readiness, but put away until needed.

From infancy to death, creepies are useful and practical, and they have a kind of rough beauty which comes from their pleasing shape, even if their construction is crude. The best creepies are as smooth as silk, with expertly planed wood, but I like the old creepies best, with worn corners and edges.

Other furniture made on the island is interesting too. There are miniature chairs for children, made with arms and curved back, exactly like the adult version. Solid and low, with a comfortable, wide seat, just right for a small cushion, they were sometimes painted red, or another bright colour. Often they were partly made from wooden Sunlight Soap boxes. The wooden sofas, with their graceful curved arms, are the same as Swedish and Norwegian kitchen sofas.

Blanket kists are in every home, each with a small drawer inside, and smelling of camphor and mothballs. I love the old kists with their dovetailed joints, useful for so many things. Some have names written inside, many are painted dark red, or green, but the beauty of the wood is seen best when the paint is removed. Dressers were also made on the island, both two and three door. None of the furniture has the finish or elegance of antique pieces, but they are solid and well-made, plain and simple in design, and in keeping with their purpose and place. But the creepie is definitely my favourite, small and neat, and just right for having tea in front of the fire.

Lights at night

LAST night we went to the pier to fetch the sludge gulper. It had been landed on the pier by the steamer, which came a night early, because of the weather forecast, so that the week's cargo could be brought in before it was too rough to make the trip. There were gale warnings for Viking, Faroes and Fair Isle, up to storm force ten.

The sludge gulper has been sent out by the council to empty septic tanks, and we had to couple it up to the tractor and drive it up to the road, before the storm sent waves lashing over the pier. There was no hint of the weather breaking up when we went down on the lorry. The sea was still and dark, with not a ripple on the water. More than four miles away, the lighthouse beam was reflected in the bay, as it swung round every ten seconds, and at the end of the pier the navigation warning light revolved red in the dark.

Everything is changed at night. The last time I was at the pier, the new community centre had just been opened, and after the dance, the hundred and fifty visitors were piped off the island on the *Orcadia*, all her lights blazing, and her whistle blowing.

But last night, with the sheep on the shores, and the

sleeping seals, we might have been on an uninhabited island, no lights were to be seen from the pier. The smell of the sea slapping against the stone steps, and the fresh wet seaweed is much stronger at night. Even the grass has its own damp fragrance. Pale fields of oats seem covered in a layer of snow in the moonlight.

Holland House, overlooking the firth, is black against the sky, windows empty and blank. No-one is there, so the flagpole on the tower is bare. People once believed that the house was haunted by the ghosts of two young children. The garden is full of birds in the sycamore trees. Fuschia bushes dropping scarlet and purple bells all summer smother the old stone walls, and laburnum casts its yellow petals. In spring there are banks of snowdrops, primroses and bluebells in the tangle of bushes, growing in the shelter of the walls. In winter, bare branches push their way between the stones, like the hedge of thorns in the enchanted forest. Tall New Zealand flax, and clumps of pampas grass survive winter after winter in the garden. An ancient bronze cannon points out to sea, the only troops in sight a herd of black cattle.

We pass the white painted wooden gates to the kirk, with its square tower, and the kirkyard beside it, full of lichened stones, many long past deciphering, some with raised kerbstones. In spring it is full of narcissi and bluebells, growing in wild abandon, transforming it into a garden. Lily of the valley grows in one corner, and moss covers old stones. Behind the old kirkyard is the new council burial ground with its straight lines. Both are referred to euphemistically as 'west of Holland'.

It is an ancient site, used for worship and burial for thousands of years.

The headlights pick out the white tails of rabbits scuttering across the road into holes in the dykes, and we slow down for hedgehogs ambling slowly along. It is surprising how many are killed on the roads even here. They are intent on their own affairs, nose to the ground, snuffling through the grass, ignoring cars and watchers.

There are bright lights further on, where a new shop is being built beside the airfield, with the island's only traffic sign – Beware of low-flying aircraft. The doctor's house is cheerful, with its lit windows, and most houses here in the centre of the island have their outside lights on. When a family leaves, or an elderly person dies, the darkened house always leaves a gap in the bright chain of lights across the island. From the dim, flickering oil lamps in the low shelters of early man, the house lights have kept out the dark night with its fears and shadows. Even now, the living lights of lamps and candles are always waiting, ready to light if the generator breaks down.

The lighted windows of our neighbours' house, and our own, shine out warm and welcoming across the loch, as we drive back to the north end.

Summer cattle

ALMOST all the cows are away from the house now, to their summer quarters. Only one black cow is left here with her calf, and she will be moved this week. I miss the red and white heifer. She was in the yard below the dyke, and always came to the dyke when she saw anyone go past, and she rattled a pail to let us know that she wanted some water. She liked to stand and have her ears and curly red poll scratched, and she is the best-natured cow we have, but her future depends on whether she can be put in calf or not. It looks as though she is going to be farrow, which is a shame.

The cattle move with such grace, walking slowly along the path by the loch, swinging full udders, and taking an occasional bite at a clump of dandelions, their coats glossy in the sun. I like the shape of their heads, their neat hooves and lustrous dark eyes, with their long lashes. None of our cows has horns, because they are mostly beef cows, though some have dairy blood. It is easier to work with polled cattle. There are one or two beautiful red cows on the island, with horns, but not many are left now.

All the cattle are different, and have their own characteristics, only noticed if time is taken to watch them while they are eating. Some are cunning, and always steal their neighbours' hay. They are adept at putting their heads into the next stall and removing great mouthfuls, sometimes while the hay is being eaten. When they have taken most of their neighbour's, they begin on their own. They know not to eat their share before committing their felonies. Sometimes two thieves are next to each other, and they forestall theft by butting. Others never seem to think of stealing.

Some are definitely more intelligent than others. Most are well-behaved, and lift their feet carefully, when being cleaned out. They seldom need a word to make them move over. Cows can be extremely crafty about kicking. They aim their hooves with devastating accuracy, and try to take you by surprise, and a large, heavy cow can deliver quite a kick. They also use their tails as weapons, and will slap you across the face when you sit down to milk, if they are not used to hand-milking, or have something wrong with their udder. It helps if someone holds the tail firmly, but the cows will stand very still for a few minutes, then give a sudden violent jerk. Cows are addressed as lass, for gentle persuasion, or woman, for exasperation.

Most cattle are in fenced or dyked fields, but where there are small rigs of unfenced grass, the cows are moved two or three times a day, like strip grazing, to eat down the grass. A long iron stake is knocked into the ground with a heavy stone, and after a few hours, the top is given a few hard knocks on either side to loosen it, and hopefully the stake comes up, and the cow is moved to a fresh part.

It is a good way of using up every available piece of ground, but it is time-consuming. Where the ground is hard, and the rock just under the surface, it is difficult to find a place to hammer down the stake, especially if a six-hundredweight stirk is charging around at the other end of the chain. If the ground is soft and muddy, a cow soon realises that she can tug up her stake and pull loose, and she will always be able to do this when she has learned the knack.

Tethered cattle need a lot to drink, and must be watered regularly, either by buckets carried from the byre, if they are near the house, or by being led to troughs. It is hard work to flit and water cows, if there are many on tethers, especially if they are some distance away.

It seems quiet here now without the cows. I can see why old people living alone often like to keep a cow; and some hens around the house, for company. If they have been used to working with cattle all their lives, it would be a wrench to part with the last one.

Days of joy

YEARS have passed since I stayed with my two uncles and two aunts on their farm in Fife, yet often the past seems to merge seamlessly with the present, as I stand again outside the open back door, in the sunshine of a long ago summer.

I go through the scullery with its stone sink, and cardboard wheel of seasonal planting dates on the wall, along the flagged passage to the warm kitchen with its range and seventeenth-century bread oven set in the wall. The old collie lies sleeping on the rag rug, and on the dresser there are lustre jugs, and spongeware bowls and mugs.

Opposite the kitchen the cold dairy faces north, and there are slate shelves where the shallow milk pans are setting for cream. There is zinc mesh at the windows to keep out flies. The wooden end-over-end churn shines with cleanliness and every week I stand with my small hands on the handle beside my aunt's, and we sing together to make the rhythm go with a swing, until the soft thud tells us the butter has come, and I am lifted up to peer through the glass porthole at the golden flecks. Soon there are plates of butter, neatly shaped by the wooden butter hands.

It is not long after the war, and an Italian prisoner of war is working on the farm. Tony Piccolo is his name, and he sings all the time. Ma Bella Margerita, and many more songs. He tells us about his family back home, and he is treated as a friend. I watch him sharpening tools at the old wheel, and he makes me a tiny silver ring from an old teaspoon. It is forbidden to take prisoners off the farm, but once I can remember an outing in the car, with Tony wearing one of my Uncle John's bunnets. He kept in touch after he was sent home to Italy, and the families remained friends.

There are horses and foals. Every evening I am lifted up on the back of one of the Clydesdales, my feet sticking out almost horizontally. I hold on to his coarse mane as he is watered at the trough, and bend my head as he is led into the stable. I love the smell of the horses, their velvet noses, and feathery hocks. The gentle whinny of the mares as they call to their gangly long-legged foals, and their joy when they run and race in the fields is beautiful. There can be trouble too, the terrible pain of the strangles disease, or a difficult birth. The horses are loved and cared for, as well as being needed on the farm, ploughing, pulling carts, all the daily work. There is still a head horseman who lives in one of the farm cottages, ploughmen and labourers.

I am free to go anywhere, except near the bull pens, or the upper floor of the barn, with its open shaft and big doors. I never go near the burn alone. But every other place is my playground, every building has its magic. I can play in the open cart shed where the carts are lined up, painted red and blue, with the farm name on the side, and Messrs J. and W. Young. I can climb up and pretend I am riding in them, or nibble treacly cattle cake in the barn. The steaming buckets of mash for the hens, full of floury potatoes boiled in the outside boiler, smell so good that I am tempted to nab a little. When the cows come in for milking in the byre I sit on the milking stool with one of my aunts and practice milking the gentle blue-grey Nell, never knowing that one day I will be milking our own cows far from here and making butter using the same butter hands.

All day is spent outside, for even in rain or snow there is so much to see and do. I can play at houses in the little stone shed, where there are pieces of broken china with pretty patterns, or curl up in the hay with one of the cats and her kittens. Every day there are eggs to collect from the henhouses. Other children live in the farm cottages, and we often play together. One of the girls is older and taller than me, and she has a doll's pram and dolls. I am scrawny and small for my age, for the time in isolation hospital with scarlet fever has stopped me from growing.

There are bee skeps at the foot of the big garden, a strange and mysterious world, where there are whole cities with queens and lazy drones, busy workers, nurses who care for the young bees, and the amazing frames which are lifted out with their load of cells filled with honey. It is a secret place, with its own unique atmosphere, full of the humming of thousands of bees, fascinating and unforgettable. The honey is so good, fragrant with the scent of flowers. Once there was bean blossom honey, from the fields heady with bloom.

In the evenings I am learning to knit and sew, buttonholing round a kettle holder, learning feather stitching and herring-bone. I can knit squares and manage a coathanger cover. On the wall is my great-aunt Margaret's sampler from Dollar School, in 1876. It says 'Remember now thy Creator in the days of thy youth, when the evil days come not', a gloomy text for a little girl. I have more fun, listening to stories, and the adventures of Bill and Ben in the *Courier* and *Advertiser.* I have no idea that these happy days full of love and kindness are going to stay with me always, giving me a safe place to revisit in the hard times which must come to all of us, sometime.

Fields of bere

THE fields of bere corn are changing colour, and soon they will be cut. Only a few houses grow bere now. It is an early and hardy form of barley, well suited to this northern climate, and with more protein and less carbohydrate than modern varieties. It is smaller, and there are fewer ears on the heads of corn, but a field of bere blowing in the wind is beautiful to look at.

In the famine years the bere kept the island from starvation. In one particular year, the people survived because they had enough seed corn to grind for food, as well as to keep for sowing for the following year's crop. There is a meal mill here which used to mill all the corn and oats, so that houses had full girnels before winter, and to make malt for brewing. The mill is one of the biggest buildings on the island, with an 'auld wife' on top, a wooden structure which helped the fire in the kiln to vent, but it was damaged recently in a storm.

Although the meal mill is no longer used, it still has all its great mill stones. There is also an old water mill, with a wooden wheel, and turf roof. Now the bere is ground in a mill on the Orkney Mainland, and everyone depends on it for what has been part of the staple diet since the first corn was grown.

Old people remember the quernstones being used long ago, to grind meal at home, and older still are the massive pot querns, where grain was pounded with heavy stones. We have one of red sandstone, which belongs to the house, and was here when we moved into it. It used to be a trial of strength to attempt to lift such a quern. Every house still has their quern stone, sometimes of granite, which glints in the sun. Some are far worn. Often they are used to tether calves in summer.

Bannocks were hard-won food, when you consider the energy needed to grind the meal. It isn't surprising that bread is something to be thought about and never wasted, or carelessly taken for granted. Corn signified life itself. The old people, remembering famine, would never allow bread to be destroyed, or corn to be left lying on the ground.

In the remote fishing and crofting communities of Norway, which are closely linked with Orkney, bere bannocks held the same important place that they still do here. The meal was mixed with water and salt, and the dough formed into round balls, and clapped between the hands into flat cakes. The right hand clapped, and the left hand supported the bannock, both hands were quick, and the cake whirled between the palms. The bannocks had to be the same size and thickness, and all the women were skilled in the art of baking them. They came in late from working in the fields and byres, and had to start then to bake enough bannocks for their large families. The hands of mothers and grandmothers were remembered, as they clapped dough into bannocks, and how the children came to the door hungry, when they heard the sound, and were given warm bannocks straight from the girdle.

Here too, the women still do exactly the same thing, and most people prefer bere bannocks to any other form of bread. Some mix them with treacle and water, and some with buttermilk, and there is white flour and baking soda in them. They are bigger than the Norwegian bannocks, which must have been of a very early kind. A stack of twelve bannocks cooling on a wire tray is a good afternoon's work. They are good with butter and cheese, or rhubarb jam, and have a slightly sourish taste, much darker than brown bread. It would be sad if the day were to come when North Ronaldsay women no longer baked bere bannocks.

Punding the sheep

AUGUST always brings a hint of the harvest to come. The light is more golden, less bright, as the sun moves west, and we move slowly across the summer path towards winter. From our house in midsummer we see the sun going down behind the sea, and now it sets below the fields of Westness. The moon was red in its last rising, and it hung, huge and glowing, in a white sea of mist. Roofs of farms seemed to float above the fog, insubstantial as a mirage. White sheep drifted like ghosts in the mist, hardly visible as vapour rose from the loch.

The punding of the sheep is still going on, with two punds daily. They are late this year, for there have to be specific moon and tidal conditions. The tide must be in, so that the sheep on the beach can be more easily gathered into the stone enclosures which are built at traditional points round the shore. Because they are territorial, and stay in their own areas of the beaches, households generally know where their own sheep are likely to be.

When the signal goes up for the pund – a large orange fishing float hoisted on a pole, which can be seen all over the island people gather at the dyke nearest the pund. The sheep are chased along the beach, and just beyond the pund, which is a dry-stane enclosure, a barrier of wire netting is stretched right down to the sea, to prevent the sheep racing past. When they are inside the pund, a temporary gate closes it off, and access is by stile only.

Sheep are recognised by their lug marks, which belong to each house. There are forty or fifty of them, and any questionable mark is referred to one of the older sheepmen, who are all experts in the subject. After identification, the sheep are sheared by their owners. No electric shears are used, because there is no power easily available down on the beach, and some fleeces have sand and salt in them which would soon blunt electric shears. Dry sunny weather makes a great difference to the speed and comfort of the shearing, and everyone is relieved when it is over for another year. It is the last remnant of communal agriculture which remains in the island, and it is unique to North Ronaldsay.

The management of the sheep is carried out by the Sheep Court, an elected body of eleven men, including the vet. They invigilate the flock, and the numbers of sheep kept by each household is regulated by the sheep regulations. Only rams with good conformation are kept. Each lamb is lug-marked by its owner, so that each animal can be identified. There are ten basic marks, the axe, stair axe, drawn hemling, stued hemling, bit, and thumb bit, the shear, the piece off, the rip, and the crook, all of which can be seen from a distance. From these basic marks, a hole, or small bit are added in various combinations, so that in the event of the ear getting damaged, it would still be possible to determine ownership. Every lug mark is recorded. The Sheep Court is responsible for ensuring that every breach in the sheep dyke is repaired as soon as possible. There is an annual count of sheep done by the sheep men and the number is recorded.

From the sea, North Ronaldsay looks like an island fortress, defended by its massive stone walls, with the thousands of sheep eating seaweed on the rocks and beaches, a diet on which they have thrived for many generations. In winter, and after the spring equinox they have an especially rich food supply, and are at their fattest. It was this convenient arrangement which ensured an adequate supply of mutton for the island through the centuries, as well as fleeces and skins, which were all used.

In summer, the ewes in lamb are brought in before lambing, then returned to the shore before a prolonged diet of grass could cause problems. They shelter beneath the dyke in bad weather, or lie chewing the cud in the sun in summer. The shore is criss-crossed with their clowgang, the ancestral tracks which they stick to at all times. They are an integral part of life on the island, and it would seem strange without them, although the work they entail, including the upkeep of the dyke, is onerous for everyone.

Return of the dark

No sooner does October come in, than my fingers itch to begin on a piece of embroidery. The drawing of the curtains before tea triggers the signal that there is a whole lovely evening at the fire, which ought to be filled with something useful and creative. Fine sewing would be regarded as a waste of time during the summer, when hard-working women should be busy outside, but in the autumn and winter, such hobbies are legitimate.

I have become more and more fascinated by needlework, and enjoy learning about it as well as doing it. I love the bright and muted colours of the threads, their soft sheen, the clean starched finish of the linen, and the slow emergence of a design which has been sewn by many women, over hundreds of years. We have been working on samplers, and someone showed me her mother's sampler from the island of Shapinsay, dated 1864. It is especially interesting, because almost everything in it is identical to the designs on Danish samplers from 1600, with exactly the same number of stitches in the peacock, symbol of eternal life, and the stylised vases of flowers, and including the same alphabets.

Samplers are fascinating to design and sew. Their designs are all symbolic, and interesting. Since this is a northern island, those I sew always have the ancient northern star, one of the oldest symbols, often seen on Norwegian knitting patterns, as well as in embroidery. The heart, cross and anchor also have a place, apple trees, a ladder, and a crown, the hart, the ship, the garland of flowers, there are many symbols to choose from. The Shapinsay sampler had the initials of thirty five people on it, grandparents, parents, brothers and sisters, cousins, all included, and each couple's initials are separated by a small heart. There is a plain, four-square house, just like the one we live in here, a henhouse with two hens, a dog with a red collar, and a black cat.

It's fun to sew samplers for new babies, or for anniversaries, and twenty-first birthdays. They are unique and special to each person, and beautiful to look at, especially if an old wooden frame can be found for them. I also love the Swedish bonads, linen or cotton wall-hangings with proverbs or well-known sayings. Their simple lines and comfortable words are appropriate for a farm kitchen like this, with its plain white walls, wooden floor, rag rug, and flower print curtains. The proverbs are always set in a garland of flowers, honeysuckle, or stylised roses and leaves. One is a stem stitch picture of two children in a harvest field, stooking the barley, which I like very much, because it reminds me of our own children, who helped in this way every year.

I have three pieces of embroidery going on simultaneously at the moment. One is a linen wall-hanging, candles and red tulips, and it is almost complete, except for the hems, which should have been sewn first. There is a scarlet table-runner, with a complicated Danish counted cross-stitch design of a lighted Christmas tree, which might prove too difficult. The last is a red heart decoration hanging on a fir branch, with a gold star beside it, on white linen. The bright red and soft green are attractive, and it is fun to sew. These winter designs bring the Christmas holidays nearer.

I like to use my mother's silver thimble, with its garland of flowers, and initials, given to her on her twenty-first birthday. I remember watching her as she embroidered the tablecloths which we use for special occasions like birthdays or christenings.

It would be good to embroider the special presents, requiring thought and preparation. Baby and christening pictures, confirmation and wedding pictures, and anniversary keepsakes are part of a well-balanced, ordered life, with time set aside for creative and beautiful work. There always seems something more needful to be done here, a sense of rush, and not much to show for it, except for a few samplers. There is something tranquil and peaceful about the patient stitching needed to make something just for pleasure.

Singing the last verse

LAST WEEK, we were listening to some of the old songs which used to be sung in the island, when people met in each other's houses, especially at New Year. Hardly any of the children or young people know them, and since they go away to school at twelve years old, they rarely have the chance of hearing them. There are no longer many left who can sing them, and the nights when they used to play the fiddle and tell old stories have almost gone, so it is a great privilege to hear some of the familiar songs.

Many of them were written to commemorate some particular event. Mining communities produced songs about pit disasters, and in coastal and island communities, the ships and fishing boats which were lost were remembered in song. The Portknockie lugger, *Evangeline*, was sunk in a gale early this century, off Stronsay:

> Built for the swirl of the wild North Sea,
> Of the toughest of oak and larch was she.
> Her masts and sails and rigging and all
> Were fitted to stand what might befall.
> But even the strongest of crafts may fail,
> In the roaring rage of an Orkney gale.

One of the saddest songs is for the *Isle of Erin*, a sailing ship which went down off North Ronaldsay in 1911, in tragic circumstances. She was lost with all hands, including the captain's wife, and two-year-old son. One old lady can remember that day and night, as she saw the lights go down under the water, and the terrible helplessness of the watchers on the shore, who had no means of sending for help, or for getting to the ship. The wreck was the means of bringing wireless to the island, so that such a tragedy would never happen again. No wonder the song says:

> Sing for the *Isle of Erin* a very mournful song.

Not all the songs are about shipwrecks. Some are the usual salutary warnings for young girls. 'The Newfoundland Sailor' was a bold deceiver, if ever there was one, when he came walking on the sand.

> He met a pretty fair maid,
> And he took her by the hand.

Unfortunately for pretty Peggy, she was left holding the baby, and her sailor wrote back to her from Newfoundland,

> You being of such low degree
> And I so very high,
> Do you think I would marry you?
> O, no, not I.
>
> But there's one thing, pretty Peggy,
> That I would have you do,
> It's take your baby on your back,
> And a-begging you may go.

And when that you are tired,
You sit you down and cry,
And you'll think upon the time you said
O, no, not I.

Most of the songs are about the sea. 'Phoebe and her dark-eyed sailor', and 'The ship that never returned', are this kind, and 'Hoy's dark and lofty isle' is about an islander who dies just before he reaches his native land. My favourite is 'The Bride's Lament', which in spite of its melancholy title, has a very attractive melody, and a good beat, with a refrain. It begins,

Long years ago, when I was young,
The flowers did bloom, and the birds they sung,
A sailor lad and his lovely bride
Sat weeping by the waterside.
It's scarce six months since I was wed,
And O how fast the time has sped,
But we must part at the dawning of the day,
When the good ship takes my love away.

North Ronaldsay's version of the ancient New Year song is now only sung by one man, and it sounds like the Faroese songs sung to a communal dance step, because of its rhythm and repetition. It consists of many verses, mostly wishing luck to the household's cows, horses, sheep, ducks, and every possible activity, and demanding food and ale for the singers, ending with threats of rough justice, if the requests are ignored.

There are many other songs which used to be sung here, which are now known by very few people. Although they have been collected and recorded, they are no longer part of a living island tradition. It would be a shame for them to die out completely, for they are really part of the island's history, handed on by oral tradition.

November nights

THE dark nights of November have come back with their sleet and driving rain hammering on the windows. No lights from other houses can penetrate these conditions. Only the lighthouse with its steady beam turns unceasingly through the night. The sea roars along the dyke, curling back in white breakers, and on nights like this, the island with its population of less than ninety truly seems very small.

One by one the farms have brought home their cattle, and the routine of cleaning out and lifting bales has begun all over again. Three long stacks are opposite the house, beside the byre and stable, their roofing hay already ravaged by storms, but a good and adequate winter supply. The cattle are hardy, and have plenty of shelter beside the stone dykes, but they are always glad to come inside for the winter.

It grows dark before four o'clock in the afternoon now, and then it is time to close the hens in, and pull out bales from the stack. Each bale is cut open, and thrown in sections to the cows in their stalls. The byres are warm and brightly lit, and the cattle are eager for their fresh hay. Often the cats come in, leaping up on the stone stall dividers, or into the space between the top of the wall and the roof, if they think they see a mouse. There are no rats in North Ronaldsay, they seem never to have been established here, and if any rat ever came ashore from a wreck it must have been quickly dispatched. There are banks mice, which live in the sheep dyke, with white fronts and of a reddish-brown colour, more sharp-nosed than ordinary mice.

By the time the cattle are cleaned out, the first stars are in the sky, and the light shining through the red kitchen curtains looks welcoming. These winter nights have so much stark contrast, the bleak cold outside, and the enveloping warmth from the kitchen range, where the kettle is always boiling, and the old clock ticks. Winter is always more extreme, where there are no lighted streets, or buses full of people all going home, and lots of noise and bustle. There is no protection against the climate, except the scattered houses and steadings, huddled against the gales and rain. When everything is done outside, and the door shut for the night, each household is an island on its own, usually with children away at school, or family grown up.

All the plants are out of the window now, away from draughts. They miss the light, and stretch towards the pale sun, and grey cloudy skies. We have ordered some hyacinth bulbs, and lily of the valley crowns to grow indoors. They are something to look forward to. Our pink and white amaryllis is growing fast. Their flamboyant trumpets are cheerful in winter. Most of our plants came as cuttings from friends, few are bought, and the house is full of them. It's fascinating to watch them grow and develop, putting out new young shoots, and they are especially welcome in winter, when their green leaves brighten the dark days.

After tea is the time when the elderly people go over events which happened long ago, shipwrecks and drownings, ancient feuds, football matches on the links, dances and concerts, accidents and sudden deaths, the coming of wireless telegraphy, and many other things which are part of the island's history. There are stories of horses, of wild cows and practical jokes, of ministers and doctors, injustice, emigration, and the press-gang. It's so interesting to hear about the days when there were five hundred people here, and life was totally different in every way. It must be sad for the old to see so many houses derelict which once were full of large families of children. Now there are more houses empty than occupied.

With the skeins of wild geese flying south overhead, and the swans coming in from Scandinavia, we are well into winter, but at least dark November will soon be past.

December days

DECEMBER is a magical month. Every year I look forward to it, rushing towards us through the winter dark, with its starry nights. Cold fingers and toes and snow showers are part of these weeks before Christmas, and ice on puddles, and breath smoking into frosty air. Snow hides the stacks beneath white dust sheets, powdering the byre roots, and melting where the warm breath of cows spirals up through the ridges. The puddles have a crazed glassy surface, thick enough for small children to slide on. Plodding doggedly through the snow, battened down in snowsuits and woolly scarves, they went to see the swans on the frozen loch, and came back, red-cheeked and exhilarated, bringing in a gust of wintry air, and leaving their boots standing in wet pools.

Silence broods over the island like a sleepy white dove. Footsteps that ring out on the stones in frosty weather, are muffled. Voices are whirled away in the snowflakes, into the grey dusk, smothered quickly in flurries of drifting crystals which sting the lips and cheeks and taste sharp and icy cold. Starlings come swirling down from the warm chimneys for crumbs thrown out to them, chattering and spreading the news, so that other birds come flocking in, hungry and noisy.

Children love to listen to fairy tales in front of the fire, and we have been reading 'The Prince and the Silver Rabbit', 'The Woodcutter' and 'The Dragon's Daughter', and other stories full of castles and dark forests, robbers and princesses. Sparks fly up the chimney, and magic carpets vanish in smoke. Mugs of hot cocoa and slices of gingerbread and butter are good after being out in the snow.

Every year we make and decorate a gingerbread house, using ginger biscuit dough, left overnight to get cold. It's fun to cut out walls and roof, chimneys, doors and window shutters, and to stick them together with caramel glaze. That's the trickiest part. The door is set ajar, and lacy paper curtains fixed in before the roof is stuck on. A house eight inches by six is a good size. Tiles are outlined with white icing, and icicles hang from the eaves. Hearts and squiggles decorate door and shutters, and a gingerbread Christmas tree stands outside. Silver balls, and slices of tiny jelly sweets are stuck to each tile, icing snow lies on window sills, and on top of the door, to make a design as much as possible like an illustration from Hansel and Gretel. When all the lights are out except those on the tree, and the candles on the table, the gingerbread house looks beautiful. I love the treacly, spicey smell drifting from the oven as it bakes, and it seems almost a shame to eat it.

We have other Swedish and Norwegian food at this time, roast lamb with red cabbage, saffron buns, and Christmas rice pudding with whipped cream and cinnamon, and one almond for luck, so good that we have it at other times as well. On Saint Lucy's day there are cakes made with almonds and walnuts, with hot coffee, and white candles on the table. Then the kitchen is decorated with hearts and stars of braided straw, tied with red ribbon. There are red striped table runners, and fat red wooden candlesticks from Denmark. The blue Christmas plate has a child carrying a sheaf for the birds, and the star of Bethlehem shines in the dark blue night. All the pictures have their crown of holly or fir, sent from the mainland, or veronica from the garden.

These four weeks are filled with anticipation, no longer with childhood's magical perception of Christmas, but with a deeper and clearer awareness of the closeness of past and present, the continuity of the generations, and the ties of love and affection which hold us tightly, and keep us safe in an insecure world.

Wind of change

THE year has begun with more violence than seems necessary. Night after night, hailstones have rattled on the windows, threatening to break the panes, and the howling of the wind has never ceased since the beginning of the month. Lightning has lit up the sky with a weird and sickly light, and thunder roars overhead, crackling on the radio, blacking out the television screen, and bringing splitting headaches. The telephone has been live, and producing phantom rings during the storms.

All round the house, continuous rain has created puddles so wide that they can be classified as lochs, with real waves. Going to barn and byre is an obstacle race, jumping from flagstone to flagstone, over thick mud. Though I hate to admit it, I left my boots at the door to dry, and they have been blown away – vanished completely. The back door and step have to be washed almost daily, to remove the build-up of salt, grit and sand, and all the windows are white with sea spray.

Trying to go round the corners of buildings is a hazard if the wind is behind you, because you are blown along as fast as you can run, or even faster, and arriving at your chosen destination is a matter of luck. Opening the door of a car is another problem, as it can be torn from you and ripped right off its hinges. Walking against the wind is almost impossible, because breathing becomes difficult.

The constant raging of wind and waves is physically tiring, and it is especially noisy upstairs, where the roof creaks and groans like a ship in a gale. Anything not tied down, or wired to cement blocks, hurtles about, leaving you wondering what made that horrendous crash. Some of these storms have been over force eleven, rising even to twelve.

On really rough days, the kitchen range hardly seems to be able to alter the temperature, as the wind sucks the heat up through the chimney. On a particularly snowy day, a dog from three miles away, at the other end of the island, opened the back door, came in and lay down at the front of the fire, on the rug. He seemed very much at home, and since then he has come quite often, sitting on the doorstep, or on the window sill, and barking to be let in.

Breath smokes white in bedrooms, unless there is a fire, so it is too chilly to read in bed. It's better to stay up late, knitting in the evenings. I enjoy this part of winter, because the soft, warm wool and the fire keep the cold night away. We have just got a Swedish catalogue with patterns for clog socks, which have hearts and cats and stars knitted into the heels. It's fun to knit jerseys with reindeers and snowflakes. Norwegian designs are perfect for winter, with blue, scarlet or dark green backgrounds, white designs, silver clasps and buttons, and woven braid. A basket full of holly-red knitting beside the kitchen fire is cheerful to look at. Rainbow jerseys are pretty, and use up small quantities of Shetland wool. Knee socks for children, with names, flowers, and snow crystals, or numbers and alphabets look good.

Soft, warm Icelandic jumpers, in brown and grey and white, are quick to knit. Fishing fleet ganseys from the home port, with the initials knitted in, are also well worth making, although the first one I made for my brother took some time. It was the Leith diamond and herring-bone pattern, in five-ply navy wool, and initials above the welt. The old people here remember ganseys being knitted on the island, plain stocking stitch, with initials on the front, then a design which had to have cables – ropes were necessary. These jerseys were sometimes used for identification purposes.

Crochet blankets are warm to make, growing cosier as they grow quickly bigger. They look so attractive, in their bright colours, with bands of black between, or white for a baby's cot. Homespun wool is especially good for making blankets, because the variety of natural colours is so great, and it is a good way of using up the ends of hanks.

Nothing makes the winter evenings pass more comfortably. Somehow summer isn't at all conducive to knitting, it's purely a pastime for the dark months of the year.

Omens

BIRTH, marriage and death in the whole of the north-east of Scotland used to be fraught with hidden dangers. There were many precautions to be taken, to avert bad luck, and there were omens everywhere.

In the cradle or in the coffin, certain rites had to be observed, and special rituals performed. At a birth, four candles were lit for the four apostles. A circle was drawn sunwise and in remote parts of Shetland, a cross was made in the air, with a knife. It was safer for boys born into a fishing family to arrive with a flowing tide, for an ebb tide meant there was a risk of drowning. A baby born with a caul was protected from death by water, and the caul was carefully preserved, because to lose it was to bring disaster to the boy. Before the cradle was used, a live coal or peat was flung into it, to cleanse it from evil influences. The same rite was observed for the baby's first bath.

It was unlucky to make many preparations for the infant, or to speak of its impending arrival. Cradles were often borrowed, after the birth, and returned with a small gift, or even a living branch, if the household was poor. To send back an empty cradle was courting bad luck. Names were never disclosed openly till after the birth, and grandparents' names were often used. However, the child was not called anything other than the bairn until after the baptism. To be forespoken was asking for trouble, leaving an open door for evil to come in. The person for whom the infant was named had to give a hansel, and neighbours who came to visit left a silver hansel coin under the pillow.

No baby was safe from evil influence until its baptism, nor was the mother, until she had been kirked. The baptism took place as soon as possible, no matter what the weather, and in this island, babies as young as three weeks were taken to the kirk in an open cart for a considerable distance, to be christened. At the baptisms were the fadders – the godparents, later called name-mithers. In Norway and Sweden, the godparents are still called fadder.

A piece of bread and cheese was often given to the first person met by the company on the way to the kirk, lucky for both the giver and the recipient. Water and the giving of a name were powerful, and the first sleep of the baby after its baptism, in its christening gown, was held to be more blessed than at any other time in life. The flickering lights of will o' the wisp in marshy land were thought to be the souls of unbaptised babies, forever barred from heaven.

Marriage too had many pitfalls for the unwary. The night before the wedding the groom had his feet scrubbed with the barn besom, and a great deal of rough treatment from his friends. The bride too had her feet washed by her own friends, and a ring was slipped into water – whoever found it would be next to marry. After the ceremony, a bride's bannock was broken over the bride's head, and children ran to pick up the pieces. The bride had to stir up the fire and put on coal, for luck in the new home. The wedding feast was always as liberal as the family could afford, and there was dancing and fiddle music. Whisky and ale were expected to flow freely. Provided the marriage took place with a waxing moon and a flowing tide, luck and prosperity would surely follow. Even today, these two conditions are thought important by the older people.

Special precautions had to be observed by a family moving into a newly built house. Often particularly significant objects were buried under the threshold, which, together with the lintel, was a magic area of the dwelling.

The sound of a cock crowing in the afternoon was though to be a bad omen, and if it occurred when a fisherman was setting off, it meant that misfortune was imminent. If a china bowl was overturned or broken, it was a clear warning. Fish bones were hidden somewhere in the house, to ensure good catches, and seaweed was also kept. Red heads and women were bad luck if met on the way to the boat, and pigeons, followed closely by cormorants on the rocks, were also unlucky. The sound of curlews crying, the 'Seven Whistlers', was an evil omen.

Death was believed to occur when the tide was ebbing, usually in the middle of the night. Life was thought to go out with the tide, just as it came with it. The dying had their lips moistened gently to make them more comfortable. On the second night after death, there was the kisting, which was attended by male neighbours and close relatives. Neighbours visited the house, to show that there was no ill-will for the dead. The dead person was not left alone in the house before the funeral.

It must have been difficult to tread warily all the time, avoiding bad luck in every area of life, in the fishing communities of the north, and even as far away as Brittany, similar customs were observed.

Back from the dark

THE tide is extremely high this morning, and the grass in the top field is under water again. When we find seaweed and driftwood inside the dyke, it makes the sea seem much too close. Foreign plastic containers, milk cartons, soft drink bottles, and a full drum of liquid deck polish have been washed up, and enough wood to keep the fire burning for some days.

The native sheep have gone up to the highest part of the beach, on the other side of the bay, and out of reach of the waves. Piles of fresh seaweed have been thrown up all along the tidelines. Not a seal is to be seen. They must all have gone round to the more sheltered side of the island, where they are safe from being battered on to the rocks.

We had Norwegian visitors this weekend, so we went for a walk to the old lighthouse, an abandoned fixed light which used to lure ships on to the rocks because of its unsuitable position. Three ships were wrecked in one night alone, last century, and countless others were lost. The old lighthouse has a large stone sphere on top, and it is a mark for fishing boats. Birds use it for roosts, and there is a large ungainly nest of seaweed on one of the sills. The houses once used by the keepers are roofless now, and it is said that the sea once came right in through the window when the keeper's wife was standing at the table baking bannocks.

All round it are the stone punds for shearing in summer, and the creel boats are pulled up there, on the stony shore. In winter the boats are taken home for shelter. On the close-cropped grass of the links are small gardens surrounded by high stone walls, too high for the sheep to jump into. There are stiles to climb over, and some are still used by the keepers for growing cabbages and other vegetables. They are very sheltered inside the dyke, but it must have been hard work to cultivate them so far from the crofts. They were fertilised with seaweed, and were of great importance to the life of the people, as recorded in the Old Statistical Account.

We looked for Halfdan Holeg's grave, mentioned in the *Orkneyinga Saga*. There is a large grave on the links, slabbed with stones, beside a sheep pund, but no Halfdan, only a few teeth and some strands of sheep's wool, a cold, bleak resting place for a king's son. Then we climbed to the top of the new lighthouse, already a hundred and forty years old, and one of the highest in Britain, with a hundred and seventy six steps spiralling to the top, as many steps as there are verses in the hundred and nineteenth psalm. It is a Stevenson lighthouse, and a beautiful building, banded with white. It is amazing that such a high lighthouse could have been built here at that time, and the first lighting-up must have been a major event for the island.

Inside it is immaculate, with shining brass, and new blue paint. The old paraffin lamp has been replaced with a 400 watt electric bulb, which is magnified many times through glass. The original fittings with their brass carvings of Greek heads have been retained.

Looking over the rail at the top, especially in a gale, is not for custard-hearted people like me. I prefer to stay inside, and read the names in the visitors' book, but the view from the balcony is incredible, because the island is so flat. It is like being in a plane.

It was easily cold enough for snow, and sure enough, it came by the time we reached the gardens of Holland House, where there are snowdrops coming out already. They are sheltered there, under the high wall and thick undergrowth. Leaves are beginning to grow on shrubs, and the escallonias are growing green. One house has Christmas roses, which have survived the freezing weather, delicate white petals above the cold ground. There are the first shoots of daffodils showing in the garden.

In spite of the cold and the storms, we saw signs of spring and there is more light in the mornings. It's still dark before teatime, but gradually the island is returning from its long journey into the winter darkness.

After the swans have gone

THERE was a stillness about the morning which was unusual, and when we looked out of the kitchen window, all the swans had gone from the loch. The night before, they had seemed noisy and excited, in fact we went outside to watch them, to see what was making them so restless. It was a clear frosty night, and the sky was bright with stars. I had forgotten that the time had come for the swans to leave the island, and fly north to Scandinavia and Russia. They were stretching their long necks, and calling to each other, the moonlight shining on their great white wings.

I wonder if it is the gradually increasing length of daylight which makes them restless, and aware that they must go. Some strange signal must trigger their convocations, and guide them back to their summer home. Their mysterious migrations are fascinating, and we watch and listen for their arrival in early winter, sure that they will come, just as they have always done.

Yesterday we went for a walk along the marshy path at the edge of the loch, and everything seemed so quiet and empty. Only a few white feathers curled on the grass were left, and what looked like an old white plastic bag, far out in the reeds. It was a dead female swan, thin and light, her beautiful downy feathers still perfectly white, and raindrops on the stretched wings. Perhaps there was too little for nineteen whooper swans to eat on this loch. They have spent so much of their time in the fields and round the byres, eating what grass is left after this wet and cold winter. It is sad to think the the dead swan is probably one of a pair and mated for life.

We always miss the swans when they leave. The constant presence of so many large and heavy birds so near the house makes winter more interesting, as they take off like an air squadron, one after another, or come in gracefully on the water. They slide on the ice, and sleep with their heads under their wings, when the ground is covered in snow.

The strong beat of their wings is a familiar sound, as they fly over the roofs, and their haunting call is the accompaniment to every day from November till February or March. It will seem lonely and silent without them. Usually a pair of mute swans nest in a clump of rushes in spring, perhaps the most northerly mute swans' nest in Britain, and they too are watched by everybody.

There is a great difference in the light in the early morning now, and I suppose that we will soon be able to do without the generator until teatime. Dawn comes just after seven, so the worst of the winter darkness is really over now, although there is snow in the ditches, and the stars are still shining at night in their winter constellations. Orion and Sirius are still glittering and brilliant in the frost.

All this month, lilies of the valley have been flowering in an old clay pot, and they have filled the house with their scent. They are beginning to fade, but perhaps they will bloom again next year, if we put the pot outside in a cold place. All the indoor spring bulbs are over now, but the daffodils outside are only an inch high, and look chewed, so they must have been eaten down by one of the native sheep, and won't flower this year.

I have been making marmalade, worth making for its colour alone. Jars of fresh orange marmalade look cheerful in this cold weather, and it tastes so good on new brown bread. There are enough marmalade oranges left to make another eighteen pounds.

The departure of the swans means that winter will soon be over, and the lighter days of spring will soon be here, with their promise of summer, but I still have a sense of loss for them, or perhaps it is really for the swift and almost unnoticed passage of time.

Seagulls and celandines

THIS is an uneasy spring, fragile as a blue glass bubble, as it floats precariously from storm to storm. Here on the island, the long silence of winter has passed, and birds are everywhere, new ones just flown in for the nesting season, and the crying of the gulls fills every waking moment. Flocks of starlings swoop and dive round the house, and chatter on the chimneys and wires, curlews and lapwings hunt for food in the bare fields, and there are nests being built in the eaves of the barn.

The daffodils came up after all, and we picked several bunches before snow blackened the leaves and gales broke the stems. They fill the kitchen with their faint spring scent, and dust their golden pollen on noses, and scatter it on the table. We put tall flower lights in a glass of narcissi for Easter, the last candles of winter. There are no wild daffodils on the island, but someone must have planted 'lilies', for clumps of narcissi come up every year on the road verges. William and I planted the daffodils one freezing winter day when he was five years old, and they are still vibrant and beautiful every springtime.

Sheltered from the bitter gales from the south-east, the celandines sit in round cushions of dark green leaves, under the dykes. I have never seen their gold enamel petals so large, in spite of the winter being so long and harsh, and the storms so severe. They are the first wild flower I learned to recognise, and I remember holding my aunt's hand as she showed me the clusters of shining petals and telling me the name, the lesser celandine.

The window sills are full of plants, cuttings growing roots in glasses of water, or being scrutinised to see if they have rooted in pots. Seeds are germinating under plastic bags beside the hot water pipes. Little pots perch precariously on big flower pots. Date stones are sprouting, baby orange trees unfolding, apple pips shooting. Two mothers of thousands have suddenly begun to throw out long streamers, and a young spider plant is producing baby spiders. Some relic of a primitive vegetation cult compels me to cover every square inch of space with greenery – geraniums, pelargoniums, sweetheart vines, elephant's ears, wandering sailors and trailing ivy, wax plants, buzy Lizzie, creeping Charlie, piggy-back plant, and the good-luck plant climb up, trail down, crawl round corners, curl along clothes lines, and tumble from every available surface, or hang from hooks in the ceiling.

Outside in the greenhouse, sweet peppers, pumpkins and cucumbers have been planted. Herbs too will grow inside its shelter, and tomatoes. The garden too is having its annual revival. By now I should know that it's pointless to dig, rake, manure a patch of sand which is first cousin to the beach over the dyke. I always forget that the pictures on the packets are not only unlikely, they are a horticultural impossibility in these conditions. Should they manage to poke their stalks up before the sand on top of them is blown away, should they even survive the salt spray which comes straight off the Atlantic, they are bitten off in their prime by marauding hordes of native lambs on their dawn patrol, or scratched up by poultry possessed of fiendish cunning and power packed wings.

The best solution is to plough out a corner of a field where the ground is good, and plant vegetables. Cabbage, carrots, turnips and lettuce will grow well. The garden is best left to hardy annuals like Virginian stock, nasturtiums, and candy tuft.

We had delicate twin calves to see to, born slightly early, into freezing weather, and their first night was spent in a large plastic box in front of the fire, packed round with hay and hot water bottles to stop their temperature dropping. They had to be bottle fed through the night, and they blorted anxiously and hung their cold ears. Sometimes lambs too have to be kept warm in the kitchen, until they revive. Calving will soon begin in earnest, as more cows come near their time. Although it will soon be the traditional date, the first of May, for turning the cows out, it is still far too cold to evict them from their warm byres. There is a cold spell in May called the coo quake, when the cows shiver and shake out in the fields, and in June a similar period when the sheep are sheared, called the yowe tremle.

This Easter the house was filled to bursting with family and visitors. Twelve of us, reading stories aloud at the fire, washing clothes in the kitchen, cooking, baking, carrying babies about, dressing dolls, making coffee, playing cards, swotting for exams, feeding cattle, mucking out byres, cutting hair, bathing toddlers, no-one can say that living on an island is quiet and relaxing.

Whole weeks disappear so fast that our feet hardly touch the ground before a month has vanished without trace.

Today the house is empty, for everyone has gone back to school and college, or driven back home to Kent and Cambridge. The silence is shattering. Only the clock ticks and the cat purrs. The sheets are all washed and airing, the bread is rising, and the dishes washed. I am glad that tomorrow we will be busy with visitors again.

Beltane fog

BELTANE brought a cold fog, and a wind from the east, bending the new grass before it had a chance to grow. The old people believe that the beltane weather forecasts the next three months, especially the direction of the wind. It's a time to light bonfires, to burn the winter's accumulations of papers and letters. The flames leap upwards, throwing sparks into the air, carrying the last of the dark months' debris off into the night. The cattle used to be driven through the beltane fires to protect them from disease and disaster, and the people danced, and carried burning torches round the fields, to help the sun on its journey into summer.

Today the fog has gone, and we are back to spring sunshine, so warm that my hands are sunburned already.

The polyanthus and primulas along the verge and in the old sandstone quern are in full bloom, a mixture of gold and crimson and yellow. The sea is still and blue, and there is a haze on the horizon. Everything smells new and fresh, the earth when it is dug over, the young grass, and in the stackyard the warm smell of sweet cicely, like aniseed, or liquorice.

This herb is called myrrh in North Ronaldsay, and its official name is myrrhis odorata. It grows beside the dyke in great profusion, and its fragrant, feathery leaves can be used instead of sugar to sweeten tart fruit, or in tisanes, but we have never used it. It must have been used in the past, because every house has great bushes of it, and it spreads and flourishes, scenting the air, especially after rain. Caraway grows here, and angelica at one time, a plant cultivated by the vikings wherever they settled.

We make no use of the plants which proliferate round the house. Dandelions and nettles are a valuable tonic in spring. Tansy and woodruff, or new-mown hay, were used to scent the clean sheets and blankets in cupboards and kists. Many of the wild plants have medicinal properties, especially scurvy grass for vitamin C deficiency. There is plantain, lady's smock, wild pansies, water mint, eyebright, cow parsley, chickweed, once used as a poultice, sorrel, herb Robert, stonecrop, and many others, all with medicinal properties. Most gardens have an elder tree, once used for a variety of troubles, berry, leaf and flower. Charms were recited to ease the pain of burns and scalds, and to staunch blood, and herbs were used, for there was nothing else. Now all the old herbs and plants are forgotten, they flower and wither almost unnoticed, their magic no longer known, or understood. But they add beauty and colour to the fields and paths, and it would be interesting to learn more about them. The kitchen herbs, thyme, marjoram, tarragon and sage, rosemary, and tall feathery dill, are homely plants. Crushed in the fingers and added to food, they are aromatic, evocative, with centuries of tradition and legend surrounding them.

The cows are finally out for the summer. They kick up their hooves and jump, pleased to feel the sun, and taste the new grass. They race round the fields sniffing the air, and find a sandy place to roll in. Already their winter coats are going, and they are looking sleek and glossy. Now that the cattle are out, the byres can be scrubbed down and their walls limed, and the doors left open to the fresh air.

The island has taken on a new aspect, and is altogether gentler, and less bleak and harsh. Young oats are up already, a green shimmer on the harrowed fields, and the nights are becoming shorter all the time. The winter always seems so long and dark, then suddenly, almost without a perceptible change, summer is almost here.

Bird week

SITTING on the doorstep in the sunshine, with a plump Rhode Island granny tucked under my left arm, painstakingly removing tar and chips from her claws with butter, was one of the unusual pastimes of the week. Luckily the hen, being the patient good-natured bird she is, clucked peacefully away to herself, while I tried to get the rapidly melting butter in between her claws. Having done the best I could with a bad job, she strolled into the tractor shed, where in spite of all advice to the contrary, and a perfectly good nesting box, she prefers a manure sack full of rolled up baler twine on which to sit, and laid a fine brown egg, a nice reward.

No sooner was my adventure with the hen over, than we were visited by a superb racing pigeon, pure white, with the merest hint of purple and green shot silk on her neck. She sits on the window sill all night, and takes corn from my hand, and sips water. She also eats with the ducks and hens, but follows me everywhere, when I go to take water to the milking cow, or rhubarb from the old wild garden.

Every day she grows more at home, and I tried not to give her too much grain, in case she forgot where she was supposed to be going. It is always a dilemma when these pigeons arrive after nights of storms and rain, hungry and light as a bundle of feathers; I have heard that they are not usually kept if they arrive back very late and so I tracked the owner of the white beauty by the ring number. 'She's been missing for months, love,' he said. 'I sent her off from Lerwick. Just you keep her for a pet, my love.' But after a few days of feeding and resting, she flew off again. I hope the black-backs don't kill her, or a marauding cat.

Yet more feathers strew our path, for when I was chasing a particularly spectacular North Ronaldsay ram, complete with magnificent curly horns, but which is a wicked delinquent, jumping over dykes to eat crops, I found that one of the young harum-scarum ducks had made a nest under the rhubarb, lined with feathers and covered with hashed up hay. There are ten warm eggs in the nest, I peeped when she was bustling into the barn for layers pellets. Another duck came squawking out of the rhubarb jungle, so there must be another nest. What a pity that although they build such good nests, ducks are such flighty mothers, trampling their ducklings, leaving them out in the rain, generally being completely useless. I've often put duck's eggs under a broody hen; they are much better at looking after the ducklings.

Hardly any fulmars have laid this year, only four in the mile or so of shore. It's sad to think there are so few fluffy grey chicks to spit at me as I go along. I always try to leave a safe distance between me and the dyke, not to alarm them too much, for they are so funny, indignant and fierce, but vulnerable to the black-backs and other piratical predators.

The grassy links are now largely covered in sand, which gets deeper every winter as violent storms blow it in from the beach. I see my own footprints as I go back and forth, keeping to the same track, below the dunes, where strand flowers grow, and a few seals loll about. I dropped my beads there, which had once belonged to a young Irish girl. My grandmother had them, and passed them on to me, and though I always look, I think I'll never find them. The sand has covered them, but perhaps one day the wind will blow, and someone else will see them, and wonder how they came to be there.

It is strange to see how little grass there is this year. No lush pastures for the cows to graze in, less milk for the calves. The rabbits, that destructive plague, have destroyed the land. The field at Sander, where recently the arctic terns nested in the long grass, is bare and there are no vicious pecking hordes to attack you as you go to check the water troughs. In spite of everything, the furry tribe continues to go forth and multiply. Here at the north end we never had them till recently, but now they are rapidly migrating towards the lighthouse.

I almost forgot that yet one more ornithological experience came my way yesterday, when I went into the old generator house where we keep the freezer. A bird was panicking and trying desperately to escape through the closed window. I caught it, and it was a beautiful tiny wren. I took it to the door to let it go, and it perched steadily on my finger. Altogether quite a week for claws and feathers.

Trip day

THE vegetable seeds are well up in the patch of ploughed field, opposite the house. It is just across the road from the garden, yet the soil is completely different, a black loam, instead of the dry sand which holds no water. Vegetables grow well in the field, and except for the time it takes to carry water out there in dry weather, it is a much more satisfactory garden. The well is in the same field, so sometimes we use buckets from it, instead of carrying them out from the byre.

Flag irises are growing tall around the edges of the loch, and marsh marigolds are everywhere. I like the flowers that grow in the damp pastures, orchids and grass of Parnassus, almost hidden in the long grass, delicately veined, and faintly scented. The cats try to catch the fat, furry bumble bees as they fizz angrily around the flowers. In the evenings, thousands of midges rise and dance in the damp evening air.

One of the brown hens has been sitting on eggs, in a nest in the barn. Unfortunately the other hens are continuing to lay in the same nest, and the hen simply abducts each new egg, raking it in under her feathers. I keep removing them, but if I didn't, the hen would soon be sitting on an egg mountain. I will have to put a barrier up to stop the others laying there.

Last week was the annual steamer trip to Kirkwall. The ship comes out the night before with general cargo, and lies off overnight. Early next morning, about six o'clock, she sails for the Mainland, calling at Sanday on the way, to pick up more passengers. It would be much quicker to fly in, instead of having eight hours in Kirkwall, and six hours at sea, but there is an almost ritualistic tradition about the trip, going back to the days when the steamer was the only form of transport, and the trip day the one day in the year when people could go to Kirkwall and back on the same day.

It's fun to be able to look in shop windows, to go to the hairdresser, to have lunch in a restaurant and go to the library. Most people have relatives who meet the ship as she ties up at the pier. There is always a lot to do, and the time goes fast – everyone has to be back on board by six in the evening.

It is a strange, quiet day for those who are left behind, to look after the cows. Getting up at four in the morning, and seeing absolutely nobody, even going along the road on a tractor, gives one an odd feeling of isolation. There is only the radio for human company. Giving the cows water helps to pass the time. It's a good day for painting a room, since there are no meals to cook, and I started to paint the living-room, but a visitor turned up unexpectedly, wanting accommodation, by the afternoon plane, so my plans didn't materialise.

The ship gets back between nine and ten in the evening, and then cars and tractors begin to come along the road, as the travellers come home with all their parcels, fresh meat, fruit, spare parts for machinery, sometimes a second-hand car, or a new television set. It is the only chance to see before buying, and then to bring home the goods the same day, instead of ordering by phone. There is something exciting about going in by sea, apart from the scenery, and the trip is usually well booked up in advance. Now that there is a regular air service, there are not as many passengers as there used to be, but the annual trip is an institution which people look forward to, and it is still an important day in the island calendar.

Now it is over for another year, and June's midsummer nights shimmer and sparkle on the sea, and make the grass grow long and green.

Scented summer days

THIS WEEK the hay is already being baled. There earth is full of cracks where the sun has dried it out. The grass is thin and poor instead of its usual lush growth. The island has changed quickly from fields blowing in the wind, to short, pale green stubble, where the birds forage for food. There are far more rabbits than usual, hopping across the road in front of cars, and sitting up on their hind legs in the sandy land, where they have their burrows.

Every day I walk along the beach, past the arctic terns' colony. They have a sentry posted near the five-barred gate which leads out on to the shore, and almost instantly the squadrons take off and begin their attack, swooping and dive-bombing, and zooming in with their razor-sharp beaks. Several times they have managed to get near enough to draw blood, but it saves time to go along the shore so that it is better to risk the attack.

Once past the terns' air base, where their chicks are just beginning to leave the hollows where they nest, the sand stretches out in a wide bay. Sometimes the sea is far out, and the wet sand is unmarked, except for ripples where the tide has ebbed, and the hoofprints of the native sheep. There are the three-toed prints of birds, casts from lugworms, and the occasional track of a seal heaving itself back into the water after basking in the sun.

When the tide is in, the seals swim along beside me, popping their heads up to see what I am doing, and turning somersaults. I usually set out with two for company, but soon there are fifteen or more.

The sheep are always munching the fresh seaweed thrown on to the sand by the tide, and they pay very little attention, lifting their heads and walking slowly away till I have passed them. There is very little drift wood at this time of year, but I did find a new rope sling which was worth picking up. The water changes colour, depending on the sky, sometimes clear and bright blue, right out to the horizon, or brilliant turquoise green. When the mist is down, and the air is full of water, the sea is a heavy grey. It glints and sparkles in the sun as it ebbs and flows, not at all like the wild seas of winter.

Coming back, I keep to the sea dyke, and the short grass below the dunes. It is longer, and slower, but warm and sheltered. Every few yards the fulmars are sitting on their solitary eggs, and spit at you if you go too near. Their fluffy offspring are plump and grey, and fun to watch as they nestle close to the wall. The fulmars are slow to take off, but once in the air their graceful flight is beautiful to watch, as they soar over the water.

In some places the dyke is incredibly high, where the sand has blown away. The labour involved in building such a monumental piece of work is amazing, and it is at its highest, perhaps ten or twelve feet there, with holes in it to let the gales blow without hindrance. Here and there are small graves covered with turf, where a dog has been buried, and the larger mounds for cows. The stone crusher, a massive piece of industrial archaeology, rusts gently away on the shore. It has a verse inscribed in the metal, giving instructions on its maintenance.

Now that the clover is out, the scent drifts down on to the beach from the surrounding fields. Everything smells of summer, and the sea makes you want to take deep breaths, especially when the sun is on the water. The warm turf has its own fragrance, and everywhere in the short grass, there are minute flowers blooming, even in the sand. The red runners of yellow tormentil are all over the links. Some flowers are so small they are barely visible, yet delicate and perfect, deep pink and starry, or white and crimson.

Inland too, the fields are full of flowers. The sandy rigs are blue with lesser bugloss, far more than usual. Red poppies, heart's ease, wild violet, white ragged robin, pink and white campion, forget-me-nots, and speedwell are growing in profusion. Lady's smock is everywhere with its pale lavender petals and sweet scent. It too must like this warm, dry weather. There is such a contrast between the seasons on the islands that we live constantly in the present, forgetting the change which comes with autumn. Summer is a time of respite, when the violence of the northern climate is tempered for a short time. The light is so bright, especially near the sea, that it makes the eyes water. It is still not really dark during the night, and dawn is around four in the morning. The birds are noisy as soon as it is light, making sure that they use every minute to feed their offspring. On these soft nights, the windows can be left wide open, letting in the scent of the flowers.

Swift summer days

THE sun and blue skies of July have filled the sandy fields with violets, shading from deep purple to pale pink, with clumps of miniature pansies in the rigs beside the coastguard watch hut. There are so many flowers there is a purple haze over the rigs. We have two cows tethered on the brae beside the hut, and it is pleasant to walk up there on a sunny evening, in the long grass, where the rabbits have their burrows. The light glitters on the water, so that sea and sky merge into one.

From the coastguard hut, we can see all over the island, with its white sand, its pale green fields where the hay has been cut, and the darker green of the oats. The heavy scent of red and white clover is almost palpable in the heat, and we have to walk through banks of it, for even the grassy track is covered with flowers, and the loch has vanished under a mass of ragged robin and pink campion. Yellow flag-irises surround the swan's nest, and there are great stretches of yellow and white lady's bedstraw, fragrant spires which fill the air with scent.

The hay is baled and stooked in groups of four, and we have been coling hay for thatching the stacks. Coling is much lighter work than stooking bales, which are at their heaviest now, before the sun and wind dry them out. I love the smell of the hay, warmed by the sun. The girls and I have to roll the heavy bales, and getting them up on the trailers is hard work. It is easier to build the loads, or to drive the tractor between the bales, and leave the loading to the men and boys. The days of raking the hay with the long wooden hay rakes are over now. This week we will have to start leading, for some houses have already got their stacks up. We have hay for three long bale stacks, and that is more than enough for the winter. In a few days, when the moon and the tides are right, it will be time to start punding and shearing the sheep, while the school children and students are still at home to help.

The hens love the sun, even though the wind ruffles their feathers and their dignity. They scratch a hollow in the old sand pit by the barn door, and have a dust bath, clucking contentedly to themselves. They are Rhode Island Red crosses, red, brown and gold, and they lay large brown eggs. Most of their time is spent in the stackyard, scratching around, and I try to carry a pail of shell grit up from the shore for them every few days. Since they are all laying just now, we have eggs to spare. 'It's a hae and a want', the old people say, because in winter they are almost unobtainable, when the cold and dark weather puts the hens off the lay.

Three long drills of onions, carrots, turnips, peas, beans and lettuces, parsley, spring onions and shallots are up and growing well now, and should last us well into autumn. The weeds too are sprouting up with vigour, though not so badly as they would in the garden at the house. Fresh vegetables are so good, straight out of the land. A bowl of lettuce with new bere bannocks and cheese is simple and wholesome.

The milking cow is producing far more milk than we can use even with a milk pudding every day, there is still plenty for the calf. There is so much thick cream on top of the milk that we have had to make butter again. Whipped cream every day is too much of a good thing, although on top of junket it is indispensable. Nobody in this house likes junket but me, and I love it. A teaspoonful of rennet stirred into a pint of warm new milk is so easy, and when it is ice cold, with a little nutmeg and cream it is delicious. Summer butter too is extra good, because its colour is a much more golden yellow, when the cows are on good green grass.

July is always in too much of a hurry to go, warm days hurtling over one another, filled with activity. These short months of summer go faster than at any other time, in spite of daylight beginning as early as three in the morning, and lasting until midnight. July 24th is the name-day for everybody named Christine, Kirsty, Kirsten or any of its variants, and today someone gave me a bunch of roses grown in their greenhouse, beautiful apricot and white blossoms, fragrant and fresh, too fragile to grow outside.

Rocky shores

ONE of the best parts of summer is the chance to go down to the beach, or the rocky west banks. The days when we can do this are few, because free time is at a premium, and it is only on the occasional evening that we can all pile into the car and drive down to the shore. The west of the island is the most popular, because the rocks are warm in the sun, and it is easy to find a sheltered place to spread out rugs, and have a picnic.

It's fun to make a fire of driftwood, and watch the blue smoke twisting upwards in the evening air. The woodsmoke and the salty smell of the sea makes everyone hungry, and children love to collect more wood. Sometimes we barbecue steaks or bake potatoes, or bananas in foil, or take a chicken casserole with us. We can drive the car right up to the rocks, and carry plates and cutlery in a couple of baskets.

There is something comfortable and peaceful about sitting with your back against a warm rock, watching the sun going slowly into the west, while the meal cooks, and the gulls swoop and dive into the water. This place is good for children, with wide, flat rocks, and no steep drops where they could slip and fall into the sea. The gulls soon realise that we are eating, and come in close for scraps, quite boldly. There is a good view over the firth to other islands, blue in the summer distance, and seals swim close to the shore.

This is an island of contrasts, and the coast is completely different from the gentle beaches and sandy bays of the east. Further round from the place where we usually have our picnics, there are deep geos of heavily stratified rocks, which fall sharply into the sea. Even on the quietest day, the tide thunders in, dark green and frothing, leaving great foaming vats of spume. The steep fissures which drop sheer to the water are terrifying, and I feel dizzy, perched on a shelf above the sea. The sucking roar as it crashes over the boulders, sending spray sparkling up into the air, is too dramatic and violent. The massive outcrops of rock are disturbing in their witness to colossal upheavals, in some primitive convulsion. There are gloups, and narrow bridges of crumbling rock, and hidden under a long cliff is the dark cave where men took refuge from the press gang.

The cave goes far in under the rocks, and smells of seaweed and slime, for the tide goes right in, and the shingle is covered in slippery weed. There is a strange, gloomy feeling about this cave, as if it retains some of the despair of those times. It must have been desperate to have had to hide here, and to have to try to get food without being seen.

Above the rocks, there are the long flat links of close-cropped grass, where sheep graze sporadically, and the sheep dyke is far inland. This place is much bleaker than the rest of the island, exposed to all the gales and salt spray of the Atlantic, and the rocks are blasted smooth by millions of years of storms.

Here and there, in the crumbling earth above the sea, are fragments of pretty spongeware pottery from long ago, soft blues and rose pinks, jug handles, pieces of patterned bowls and deep saucers, once dumped on the rock face. It's interesting to pick them up, and see how many of the old patterns are there. Spongeware was made in the Glasgow potteries and imported by sailing ship in the last century.

A week ago, we went for a walk with a Norwegian friend, who has an oil painting of Ryas Geo. She wanted to see this rock formation for herself, and we sat on the cliff for a while, watching the sea and the birds. Cormorants always gather on the outcrops and skerries, and black guillemots preen their feathers. The cormorants hang out their wings to dry, standing with them stretched out wide, to let the wind and sun dry their feathers.

On the way home, we gathered driftwood, bleached and strangely carved by the sea. It's always interesting to wonder where it has come from, before being washed up by the tide. We should try to find more time to go to the beach. Sea pinks cling precariously to the cliff tops, as evanescent as the short weeks of summer, vanishing now into the autumn mists.

Passing ships

HARVEST lightning has been flickering across the sky, hairst blinks which come only at this time. Sometimes Saint Elmo's fire can be seen on the hands, when you are pulling bales or sheaves out of a stack, or feeding them to the cattle. It flashes blue round the arms, and it was sometimes seen round the rigging of a ship in a thunderstorm. Depending on your preference, it could be either a sign of Saint Elmo's protection, or a portent of disaster.

The most alarming form of lightning that we have had here was a ball of fire, which seemed to shoot in through the kitchen window during a very severe storm. It was about a foot in diameter, and exploded with such a bang that it shook the whole house. The telephone was live afterwards, and all the fuses blew in the local exchange. Blue forked lightning continued to flash across the room for several hours, and the back melted off a radio.

Thunderstorms are infrequent, but spectacular, here, where there is such a wide sky, and flat horizon. Cattle have often been struck and killed, tables split in half, people stunned, or occasionally killed. One of the huge standing stones in the Ring of Brodgar was smashed by lightning. It is always a relief when the last rumble of thunder dies away, and rain starts to come down to freshen the air.

The last sheaves in the island are in now, and the year's outside work is done, apart from the potato harvest. This is a pleasant time of year, when the moon is large and red, and fields lie peaceful and quiet after their year's cycle of growth. The days are clear and blue, with a crisp brightness which comes at no other time.

Mushrooms grow in the stubble, and the last white roses are on the old sweet briar bushes in the garden. The cattle are still out in the fresh grass growing where the stooks have been lifted. In one field the ground is covered with a second crop of heart's ease. I don't remember seeing so many at this time of year, but perhaps it's just that I didn't notice them. They are supposed to have been used for insomnia, coughs, and tuberculosis, as an eyewash, and mouth wash, and as a compress for reducing swelling, as well as for sore throats, heart disease, gout and arthritis.

Up at the coastguard hut there is an old ruined croft where fulmars nest in summer, and from there you can get a clear view of the sea. Because this island is on the North American route from Scandinavia, there is constant traffic going back and forwards, container ships, tankers, trawlers, and in summer, the cruise liners. There is often a line of fishing boats going south from the fishing grounds, but no longer in the numbers which used to sail past, or shelter in the bay with their mast lights shining all night.

Sometimes there are yachts taking part in a race, or on a pleasure trip. Seen through the binoculars, they are fascinating and graceful, as their sails billow out in the wind. One of the students who has stayed here has twice come to visit us with her family in the yacht *Mhairi Bhan*, and we have been able to watch her progress almost from the Fair Isle, as she made her way south to North Ronaldsay.

It must have been beautiful to see the old sailing ships as they raced past the islands. Occasionally a training ship goes past, and we can catch a glimpse of what these ships must have looked like. There must have been a great many coming and going, considering the number of wrecks. The skill needed to sail these ships in the dangerous waters with their hidden reefs and currents, and sudden storms, must have been phenomenal.

There are still some creel boats going out, until the weather breaks up, and it becomes too hazardous for small boats to be at sea. Very few boats are left, as bigger boats come in close from outwith the island, and catch the lobsters which were traditionally the preserve of small island boats. Most days there are fishing boats taking up creels round the shore.

The sea provides us with constant interest, and everyone watches the horizon to see unusual ships or oil rigs sail past, during the day, or lit up at night, in stormy weather or fine.

Autumn rain

NECKLACES of starlings are strung along the hydro wires, and on the stone-flagged roofs of barn and byres. The sky is black with their murmurations. Wild geese are flying south, their haunting cry echoing as they cross the island, warning us that winter follows at their tails. Its cold breath has already blackened the clover and shrivelled the stubble.

Flocks of birds come in every day, colourful strangers blown off course by the wind, and the familiar travellers, wheatears and redstarts, which fly in every autumn and rest in the fields before their long journey. Once, hundreds of swifts flew in, misled by thick fog, and the air was full of their wings, as they settled on dykes, roofs, even on outstretched arms, beautiful and breathtaking. An owl watches us from a fence post, eyes glowing in the dusk like lamps.

There is a wild salty smell from the sea, and far out the breakers on Seal Skerry forecast a change in the weather. The native sheep are all back on the shore again, after their summer on the grass, and each stormy tide throws up more shiny wet tangle on to the beach for them to munch. They soon grow fat on this healthy diet. All the shearing is finished, and the sacks of fleece, grey, black, tanny and white, have been packed and shipped.

The young fulmars I have watched every day since they were in the egg are flying now, and have left their sandy hollows under the dykes. Many birds use the ancient archaeological sites for nesting, where the Iron Age people once scanned the firth for raiders.

The last sheaves have finally been brought home to the stackyard, a late harvest, and the fields are bare and empty. For weeks the stooks stood shock-headed in rain and wind, in sunshine and moonlight, golden chains stretched across the low hollows and slopes of the fields. No season is more satisfying than this, the year's work complete and the stackyard full.

The hay harvest was the wettest anyone can remember. Every day the rain saturated the crop, and several times the waterlogged coles had to be knocked over and raked through, moved to a different patch to let the wind dry them. Twice they had to be pitched over again, leaving circles of blackened grass and pale bleached roots. Instead of warm, dry sweet-scented hay, the loads on the trailer were damp and sodden. We were lucky to save as much as we did, and at least the weather improved in time for the oats to be harvested.

This year we have no cows to send away. Our heifers are being kept for cows, and the familiar matrons are all going to come into warm byres for winter, until the spring calving. I love the cows, they are all calm and good-natured, a joy to care for, especially as we still have a milking cow, Peggy.

Every day for weeks there have been at least a hundred seals in the bay below the house, swimming and turning somersaults. Out on Seal Skerry the grey seals have their pups, and we can see them through binoculars when they lie up on the rocks. It would be sad if the current seal virus were to reach the island. It would seem strange and empty without their constant company and calling, although they are a nuisance for fishermen. North Ronaldsay people are known as selkies, and it was the code name for the island during the war, to relay information about steamer sailings.

These are the last few weeks before the darkness of winter, and we put off lighting up for as long as possible, to make the day last until the sun sets and the evening star rises. Soon we must batten down the hatches and wait for the storms, for the summer passengers, like Victor Hugo's swallows, have gone south.

'Oh! c'est triste de voir s'enfuir les hirondelles! Elles s'en vont là-bas, vers le midi doré.'

Cargo of drift

WE had a tremendous storm last Tuesday night, reaching force eleven, and gusting to over seventy miles an hour. It tore the tops from stacks, and ripped doors off sheds. I went out for some coal, and was blown right across the road into a stack, and it was a struggle to get back into the house. The pail went flying out of my hand, and was retrieved next morning on the other side of the field. The men had to tie down the stack nets even more firmly, weighting them with heavy scrap iron, but by the next day the worst of the storms had abated temporarily.

That night, in bright moonlight, thousands and thousands of pine logs, about three feet long, were being washed up round the islands, deck cargo washed from a ship carrying wood for pulping. It was a strange sight to see lamps and torches bobbing up and down on the rocks, as every man, woman and child went clambering down to the sea in the dark, to bring up the wet logs, and heave them over the dykes into the fields, or stack them in piles above the tide-line. They were heavy to carry, saturated with salt water, and cold, smelling of resin and seaweed, and it was no easy task to lift them out of the water and carry them up the steep slope to the dyke.

The five children who were with us were hauling up logs as fast as they could, gripped by the ancient acquisitive fever which attacks everyone on a hunt for driftwood. Log after log came hurtling over, and the cattle in the field became excited by all the lights and activity, and started to bawl loudly. It was easy to trip over logs in the darkness, and many were far out on the rocks. The moon cast long shadows, and it was exciting to be out on the shore with so many other people all gathering drift. Dim figures loomed out of the darkness, and lights flickered and disappeared behind the point.

After two or three hours, and well past midnight, we were ready to go back to the house for hot coffee, but all night people were going back and forwards to the bays and inlets with tractors and cars, for nothing like it had been seen since the wreck of the *Gezina* in 1925.

Next morning at first light we went to look over the dyke, and even more logs had been washed up overnight. Logs were lying in pools left by the ebb tide, everywhere along the beach. It was much more awkward to pick them up, because the rocks were covered in slime, and the wood was heavy and wet. Although people had been working all through the night, there were still more logs floating in the sea, tangled in the seaweed, while up on the grass lengths of timber were scattered all along the fields above the sea.

The planes reported seeing great rafts of driftwood floating out at sea, a hazard for shipping, and every day more is coming in, to be picked up and carted home. It is incredible to see so much timber everywhere on this treeless island. At least some of it will help to keep us warm this winter if it is chopped up, or perhaps it could be used for fencing. The lengths are too short for anything else. It has been confirmed that it was deck cargo, and that nobody was lost overboard on such a terrible night, for such a fear is never far from anyone's mind during the winter storms.

All week the gales have continued, rising to force eleven again, and bringing hail showers which tore horizontally across the island. Saint Luke's little summer has gone without trace. It's time to bring the cattle home, before winter comes raging down from the north.

Thymes past

THE last traces of autumn have vanished, whirled away by a storm from the south-east. The grass has changed from green to bleached grey, and the bushes of sweet cicely in the yard have seeded and turned brown, feathery leaves curled and withered. Tansy with its dull gold buttons and strong scent grows round the house. I meant to pick some to dry, and hang in the linen cupboard, but it is too late now.

I wish that southernwood could grow here in the garden. I love its clean astringent fragrance, and silvery green leaves. My aunts called it apple-ringie, and it grew in abundance in their garden, among the crimson clove carnations, damask roses, bergamot and lavender bushes. Red and white striped roses of York and Lancaster, and tall bushes of white marguerites, low conifers and a monkey puzzle tree, made the garden a fascinating place for a child.

I loved the sweet-smelling herbs best, the clean pungency of thyme, warm lemon balsam, where the bees buzzed, grey green sage, and spiky rosemary. I crushed the leaves in my fingers, and the scent still takes me back to that sunny garden.

In the sitting room, pink rambler roses nodded and tapped on the windows, and wallflowers in the flower bed below sent their sweet smell drifting in. *Queechy*, and *The Fur Trappers*, and many books from long ago were in the bookcases, and there was a wooden solitaire board in the drawer of the sideboard. I played Chinese chequers, or picked out 'Let the proud Indian boast of his jessamine bowers' on the piano.

The summer house smelt of sun-bleached cushions, and warm paint, and there was a shed in the steading with a collection of broken saucers and cracked cups with pretty patterns, and discarded pots and pans to play with. The dogs, Sweep and Dick, were good-natured, and there were the barn cats, Sandy who had been through the threshing mill, and survived, Fluff and her kittens, and many more. I could watch the ducks on the stackyard pond, fetch the cows home for milking, and have a mug of frothy warm milk drunk through a clean straw from the stack. There were eggs to collect, and the ten o'clock piece to carry to my uncles in the fields, while my aunt carried the scalding pitcher of tea.

In spring there were wild daffodils on the grassy banks, much smaller than garden daffodils, with a sweet smell, and pollen which blew out in a golden cloud, dusting your nose and making you sneeze. Honeysuckle twined among the dog roses in the hedges, and frothing meadowsweet and queen of the meadow lined the ditches. The old stone wall at the back door was a garden in itself, with yellow stonecrop and wallflowers, and miniature plants growing out of every crack.

Rows of raspberry canes, redcurrant and black-currant bushes with their bunches of jewelled berries, goose-berries with sweet yellow globes, and hard green fruit for jam, strawberries and brambles were allowed to be picked, and young peas in their pods. There were apple trees in the orchard, where the washing blew in the wind, and pear trees against the sunny wall.

As though they had been recorded on film, the warm sunny days are still there, clear and bright, with their flowers and scents, kind hands and voices. I crush a geranium leaf, and am back in the kitchen, sitting on the blue and red rag rug, in front of the black range. The dog is asleep, twitching his paws as he dreams, and a kitten purrs. There are red geraniums in the window, and the smell of baking, as a scone is turned on the girdle.

I have learned to read, and am learning 'Friendship' and 'A little city, worn and grey' from the poems on the mantelpiece, and 'Immortal, invisible' from the hymn book, incomprehensible but majestic. 'We blossom and flourish, as leaves on the tree' is what has attracted me. 'God is Love' is another puzzle, which I see painted in gold letters above the pulpit in Kinglassie Kirk, a mystery which I do not understand, as I sit in the wooden pew, feet swinging, between my two uncles, although all the time it is being translated for me in human terms.

In the evening the lamp is lit, and there is the faint smell of paraffin. The uncles sit by the wireless, listening to the news, and reading the *Courier.* Nobody sits up late, when cows have to be milked early in the morning. I see the pattern on the red stair carpet, and the wide, curved bannisters, as I climb upstairs to the blue room, with its dark blue button-back chair. I am not at all afraid of the dark, for one of my aunts sleeps in the same big room, and outside the stars are shining. I know some of their names, and can find the Plough, and the Hunter with his dog, striding over dark hills in winter.

The senses of childhood are so acute, and perceptions so interconnected that sounds and scents and textures are inextricably bound. A drift of fragrance, and we are back in the bright bubble of the past, where nothing could change, and we thought that we were safe forever. In an instant of time, days and weeks, with their sunshine and rain, familiar voices, and rooms once known, are as real as this island kitchen, and we are enclosed in their loving magic, playing tricks with time.

Lighting up time

YESTERDAY North Ronaldsay was switched on to the national grid, after years without mains electricity. At last we have caught up with the rest of Scotland. The power comes through five submarine cables into Nouster Bay. There was a reception for the entire population of the island, and many visitors flew out for the day.

For the past month there has been constant activity, as the hydro poles and cables have gone up. A helicopter brought the poles from where they had been landed at the pier by the ship, and laid them one by one at the side of the roads, or across fields. Each pole took approximately three minutes to bring. Some rocky places had to be dynamited so that the poles could be put up, and it was fascinating to watch the speed of the operation. It took only a day to lay the submarine cable across the firth.

The poles have given perspective to the roads, and make the flat landscape more like the rest of the country. It would have cost a phenomenal amount to put the cables underground. The fact that the power links us to the rest of the Mainland is a tremendous boost for an island which has always been isolated and remote. There is a hydro pole just outside our house, over the garden wall, with its transformer. The cable goes under the garden, through the wall below the window, under the wooden floor and below the stairs to a meter on the wall. I think all the poles should be flying flags, for the power will really bring North Ronaldsay into the twentieth century, and will make tremendous changes for the better for all of us.

Life here is physically very tough, not only because of the severe weather and prolonged storms, but because there are not really many able-bodied people left on the island. Winter in the north is especially long and dark, and light has been man's only weapon against it. Being able to switch on lights at any time, without having to start up the generator will be a fantastic help.

Nobody takes light for granted here, because generators have to be maintained, spares are difficult and expensive to get, and oil has to be ordered from the Mainland. It costs roughly four times as much to have power by the generator as it does by hydro-electricity, so bills should be much lighter. Only twenty-five per cent efficient, the old generator chugs away all evening to keep the lights and television going, as well as the electric blankets. The iron can only be used if the outside lights are switched off, and never if the washing-machine is on. We never use the immersion heater, because it is too heavy, and makes the lights dip.

The help that the hydro will bring is incalculable, for every aspect of life will change here. When cows calve at night, there will be no need to switch on the generator, or light a stable lantern. Byres can be lit for suppering cattle in winter and on dark mornings. Breakfast television will even come to North Ronaldsay. Deep freezes will be easy to operate, without the need for a small generator especially for them, or a regular number of hours on the big generator. Frozen food is a very expensive luxury here because of the price of oil, yet almost every house has to have a freezer, to make it possible to keep food fresh from steamer to steamer, from a week to ten days, or longer in stormy weather.

One of the best benefits which the hydro will bring is the comfort and well-being of the elderly. Most don't keep their fires in all night, because of the risk of fire, a disaster in an island, and their only light is gas or oil. Being able to put on the light if they have to get up at night, especially where there are stairs, will be much safer. An oil lamp tipped over by accident would be a nightmare. Electric blankets will mean warmer and drier beds in houses which hardly ever have damp-proof courses.

The thought that washing can be dried now in a tumble drier is marvellous, after years of stormy, wet weather when damp washing has had to be dried inside somehow. A heated towel rail in the bathroom will make life much less spartan here. Where there is no power, there is no point in wishing for fridges or mixers, or automatic washing machines, but now we can really enjoy the benefits of electricity, having known only too well what life is like without them. I had begun to believe that there would never be mains electricity in North Ronaldsay, but the E.E.C. provided the grant to bring the island into the modern world. The arrival of the power certainly deserved a great celebration.

Winter solstice

DURING the solstice, the sun seemed to stand still. The Norsemen kept the twelve days, from 22 December, as the festival of yule, and all work involving a circular action ceased. The flail was not used, nor the rotating quern stones. Cart-wheels, spindles, all were still. In the remote northern isles, occupied for centuries by the people of Western Norway, yule has always been a special time.

At the turn of the century, the low stone houses were outwardly silent and dark in the biting wind, but inside there was noise and bustle. The rooms had all been cleaned, Christmas cards set up on the dresser and mantelpiece. Crisp oatcakes had been baked on the iron girdle, and bere bannocks big as soup plates, dusted with meal. A pig had been killed when the moon was waxing, and there was pork to fry, and good white lard. Bacon was curing, salt herring filled the barrels, and mutton from the yule sheep was boiled. There were mealy puddings in the girnel. A woman's reputation depended on the mutton and bannocks provided for neighbours who came to bring in the New Year. There was cheese too, and butter, the best each house could provide.

Outside in the barn and brewhouse, the men, and sometimes the women, had been busy brewing ale. There were ancient superstitions concerning this particular brewing, but they had disappeared. At one time in Scandinavia, crossed sickles were fixed above the brewhouse door, and a silver coin or ring was placed in the brewing vessel. No steel or knives were used. During the fermentation, extreme care was necessary, the process had to be helped by yells, and singing. In North Ronaldsay, malt was made from bere corn. It was threshed and dressed, steeped in water, dried, spread out on a stone floor, and turned. It was dried in the kiln, winnowed, cleaned and crushed. Then the malt was ready.

It was put in a big wooden vat and covered with boiling water for two hours, then the wort was drained off. This liquid was boiled for two and a half hours, then strained and cooled. A little was mixed with yeast, to start it barming. The ale was finally bottled, and left to clarify.

Yule was the season when relatives at distant crofts were visited. A small girl at that time was bathed in the wooden wash-tub, her long hair washed in soft water and dried at the fire. It was tied up in strips of white rags the night before. Her petticoats were crocheted in pink and white wool, her chemise was hand sewn, and she wore long black woollen stockings, and square-toed shoes. She had a home-made skirt of thick navy serge, and a white long-sleeved blouse with pearl buttons.

Horses were not usually harnessed at night, and the lantern was lit for a journey on foot, or visits were made when the moon was bright. In the firelit kitchen it was warm and bright in the soft glow of the paraffin lamp hanging from the ceiling hook. It was exciting to sit at the table, with its wedding china, polished spoons, fruit cake, and 'cakey shortbread' from the Mainland, with icing on it.

At a time when Christmas was celebrated less than New Year, it was interesting to hear that this particular child hung up her stocking on Christmas Eve, and got a doll, an orange and an apple, a shilling, and sweeties. A neighbour who went to Kirkwall every year for the Lammas Fair always brought back a doll for the Christmas stocking. The laird's wife at Holland House had a Christmas party for all the island children, with a tree. Each child was given a number on a slip of paper, and each got a present with their number on it – a sewing set, or a tiny rigged sailing ship.

Hogmanay was the most important day, with its own customs. Every woman did a big washing, so that no dirty clothes were in the house for the New Year.

The floor was swept inwards to the fire, so that luck wasn't swept out of the house. The men of the township met on the evening of Hogmanay, and visited each house in turn. They were given mutton, bere bannocks, oatcakes, cheese, and as much ale as they could drink. Sometimes the ale was heated on the fire, with sugar, and poured foaming into a pottery ale can. Old ballads were sung, and there was plenty of noise, singing, eating and drinking.

The celebrations went on for several days and nights, bringing a bright light into the darkness of winter, something to look forward to, and to remember afterwards.

The fires of January

AT LAST the cold, pale sun of early January has managed to cast low shadows on the house wall, as it moves westwards to set in the afternoon. Since Christmas Eve, the most ferocious storms have roared around the island, making it too difficult to talk, or to listen to the radio or watch television. So violent was Christmas Day that we were sure that the windows facing south-east were going to blow in. Hail and sleet have hammered relentlessly and there is a thick encrustation of salt on window panes and paintwork, which must be washed off, but not yet.

Such desperate weather lasting for so long is unusual. It has been so severe that the present force eight seems like a gentle breeze, after the force twelve and force eleven we have been having. There are stretches of dyke down, and stacks damaged. Fields and steadings stand in water, for there has been much rain. The island is scoured clean and fresh, its rocky bones bared by constant abrasion and there is no shelter anywhere from the icy sea spray, which fills the air, and stings the lips, leaving the taste of salt. The gales slash the cheeks almost to the bone, filling the eyes with water.

Only the sheep on the rocks are unaffected by the storms, sheltering under the lee dykes. The high tides produce great quantities of seaweed, so that they have an increased diet in winter, and grow fat. In the worst of the weather a gate is opened to let them in off the shore. This stormy weather is eerie, especially during the long hours of darkness, when the chimneys roar and the roofs creek, and the sea churns and foams white, pouring over the dyke into the yard. Such violence is completely uncontrollable, and becomes exhausting after weeks of constant noise. Like packs of wolves howling down the Arctic wastes, the wind snuffles and claws at the door, trying to force its way in.

October's pitprops, washed up by the thousand, have been providing extra fuel, burning every night in the downstairs bedroom fire. They are three feet long, so there is no need to chop them up, as they burn quickly, and can be pushed further into the fire as they burn. The flames throw soft shadows on the walls, and toes on the fender keep warm. Storms outside make the firelit room a fortress, with its thick stone walls. There are hardly any outside lights in the island now that electricity has come, so that ironically it has made the nights much darker. When generators were used, powerful lights shone from barns and byre roofs.

No wonder that so many superstitions and rites for New Year are of a sinister or frightening kind. Who would want to come through to the kitchen on New morning to look for an imprint of a human foot in the ashes, toes pointing towards the door? A newly-lit peat or coal rolling away from the fire was just as unlucky. Fire was an important religious symbol in the north, and was part of the ritual of New Year in the fishing communities. The burning of the clavie at Burghead on the Moray coast was one of the relics of the pagan fire festival, and a hundred years ago burning faggots from the blazing tar barrel were thrown in open doors for good luck, as the clavie was carried round the village. It used to be carried to the harbour, to purify the fishing boats of all malignant influences.

All around the north-east coast, torches were burned, and offerings made to fishing boats to drive away evil spirits, and cleanse air, earth and sea from unclean and hostile influences. Now the greatest fire festival is Up Helly A' in Shetland, held on the last Tuesday in January. The blazing torches of six hundred guizers are cast into the replica of a viking longship, complete with dragon, followed by a night of celebration.

On the Banffshire coast, it used to be the custom at New Year to go to the shore, fill a jug with sea water, and carry it home with a certain type of seaweed. The water was sprinkled over the fire, and the seaweed hung above the doors, and in the corners of the houses, to bring good luck for the rest of the year. Some of the more superstitious fishermen would not go to sea until they had shed blood. If it was too stormy to put to sea on New Year's Day, men who owned guns went to the shore to wait for a bird which could be shot. If this failed, the blood of a fish could serve as a propitiation. The first boat to reach the fishing grounds, haul in, and gut the catch, would have the best luck through the year.

It used to be thought important to begin some piece of work, fishing-gear mended, torn clothes repaired, or something new cut out, some straw rope woven, a piece of knitting begun, or a stone of a dyke set up, so that the New Year could begin with a blessing for thrift.

The old superstitions and rites have gone for ever, and the New Year song with its fifty verses is no longer sung. After the candles and bright lights of Christmas, there are still the dark, cold weeks of January and February to come. By New Year's Day there is said to be an extra hour of daylight. Only the bowl of pink hyacinths on the kitchen table, and the new green leaves beginning to grow on the pelargoniums, show a tentative sign that this cruel January will give way to a gentler time.

Encroaching seas

LIKE a soft quilt of feathers, snow has settled down on the island, quieting the storms which have raged and roared around us for weeks. For the first time since before Christmas, it has been possible to sleep right through the night without waking, as part of the roof creaks with unusual violence. Morning comes with the unmistakable blue light of snow reflecting on the white walls, and the sharp, clean scent of ice on the loch. The freezing temperatures caused by wind-chill have risen slightly with the return of the snow.

The gales have done tremendous damage. During one tide, from flood to first ebb, miles and miles of the sea dyke have been torn away. The sea roared in, meeting loch water, flooding roads, and producing a scene of such destruction that has not been approached since 1937, when there were far more people to repair the dykes. Now there are as few as fourteen men under the age of sixty, so the devastation of the dykes is really a major disaster for the island.

The waves were so huge that they were right over the store at the foot of the pier, and it was quite terrifying to look out of our upstairs windows to see waves coming in over the dyke, and at their height towering up above the roof of the house on the other side of the loch. One house was completely cut off by sea, so that the person who lives there had to leave for the night, before the second tide. It was a pitiful sight to see the henhouse standing feet deep in water, and the broken shards of dyke scattered around.

Hundreds of sheep poured in through all the gaps and ran in flocks up the roads, over the fields and round the stacks. Their hooves pounded past us as we went to feed the cattle in the byres, sixty or more sheep racing through the yard.

Since snow covers the ground, the sheep can't eat down all the grass, but when it thaws, they will be able to do an enormous amount of damage. It seems strange to see so many around, for usually storm damage to the dykes is not on such a scale.

We had to drive through the sea at one point, where it had come in and flowed into a loch. There was seaweed and driftwood floating about, and down at the old lighthouse the sea had come right in, completely covering the shore, and Dennis Loch had gone. Bridesness too had vanished under the sea, and some of the pitprops from the shore came floating up the road to meet us.

There will be a considerable change in the formation of the beaches when this is over, for at the pier all the beautiful white sand has been sucked out and away, and perhaps it will be cast up on another beach, when there are changes in the winds and tides. It seems strange to be without television, for the transmitters are damaged. It's time to pull the sofa in to the fire, and sew or read, while the soft thud of the snow blows against the windows in the dark.

The spring lambs

LAST NIGHT we began taking in the first ewes for lambing. More than any other season, this time of year has a unique facet in North Ronaldsay, a strange, primitive world of stones and flood tides, when the island is silent under a still evening sky. When tides are full, everyone goes down to catch ewes in lamb, or those already lambed, to bring them inside the dyke for the summer.

At certain points in the dyke there are stone fanks, cleverly designed with narrow passages leading into them, and off-centre openings, which trick the sheep inside, so that they can be caught. When the tide is full the sheep are easier to manoeuvre, because there is less of the shore for them to run on. The rocks are covered by the sea, so that the sheep are prevented from going out on to the ebb. There are grassy high walled quoys, or parks, along the inside of the dyke, and the ewes are lifted over the wall into them, and are soon eating grass. The old sheepmen were not short on ancient wisdom, for in certain parts of the dykes there are wide lintel stones, just high enough to let a sheep through at ground level. The packed stones are removed from below the lintel, the sheep put through, and the dyke built up again.

I would never spot these lintel stones myself. I think anyone would have to be born here to know even a little about the sheep and their lugmarks, their clowgang never deviated from, and their territorial knowledge which will take them straight back to their own part of the shore, no matter where they are released.

The old sheepman can recognise the marks even at a distance, and know who each sheep belongs to. Lambs are marked as soon as possible after birth. Our mark is a shear on the right, a piece off the left, a bit afore and a bit ahint. The lambs are much more attractive when they are first born than later on, when their early soft wool changes to fleece stained by weather and sea water. Their colours are so varied, curly soft coats, smelling warm and fragrant, black, white, tanny, and white with tanny or black ruffs. If they lose track of their mothers on the beach, they come to humans, not having seen them before, but it is never very long before the ewes hear them, and come for them, calling in the croaky bleat used only for their lambs. They follow their mothers, many of whom are aged grannies, with years on the shore behind them, teeth worn down by a decade of munching seaweed, but still agile and speedy on the hoof.

There was a heavy sea running, and white breakers out on the skerry, but it was sheltered around the punds. The two children with us helped to catch the sheep, and played beside a small loch, launching driftwood cruisers and having races with them. There is shell sand down on the shore, with rock pools full of coloured stones, and red sea anemones. Round the point, beside the old lighthouse, is the only place where there are cowries, groatie buckies, creamy-white, dove-grey, or pinky-brown. They are children's treasures, to be hunted for, exclaimed over, and collected in damp matchboxes. We found a lot of drift, broken fish boxes from Kinlochbervie, twisted branches, and planks with shells fastened to them.

So few islanders live here now that it is eerie and uncanny to be on the shore, among all the old, lichened stone walls, built so long ago, and used by so many hundreds of people long dead. The shades of ancient sheepmen must be hurrying along the shore with their ghostly dogs, catching their yowes and marking lambs, leaning up against the dyke for a yarn, and smoking their clay pipes, as they watch the tide, and the endless ebb and flow of the sea.

The sun sets huge and red, over the western rocks, leaving a rosy glow in the sky. The lighthouse comes on the moment the sun goes down, faint at first, in the twilight, stronger as dusk comes, circling the sea every ten seconds. Everything smells salty and fresh. The moon, almost full, rises in the east, high and cold, an icy world floating above the sea, and the island is still and quiet. All the sheep have found their lambs, and the first star shimmers into sight, closing the circle of the day. 'Star of evening, bringing all things that bright dawn has scattered, you bring the sheep, you bring the goat, you bring the child back to its mother.'

Mushroom weather

ALL THROUGH the damp weeks of autumn the fields have been full of mushrooms, big as soup plates, or in clumps, gleaming pearly in the long grass, and in the pastures where the cattle graze. It has been tempting to gather too many at once, for every morning more have sprung up, with rosy gills and clean untouched skins. They glow like moons in the dawn, when the cows are still half-asleep and the calves are just beginning to stretch. In some years there are none to be found, in others they suddenly appear, unpredictable and mysterious. They are an extra treat, a gift that comes at harvest time.

These wild mushrooms are full of flavour, growing in the clean salty air, outside in the grass and even in the road verges. We eat them raw in salad, or baked in the range in a little cream, or fried with potatoes. They are useful in casseroles and stews, even frozen, but best after a long hard day, just cooked for tea straight from the field, with new bread.

The oats are changing colour from green to silver, waiting for the binders to be freed from their protective covering of straw and tarpaulins. Soon the whirr of the wings and clack will be heard as the old machines cut and tie the sheaves, before storms lay the crop flat, or ravel it into a tangled mess. Already one or two rigs have been cut and stooked. The bere corn too is almost ready, though less is grown every year. This ancient crop, full of protein, has been grown in Orkney for thousands of years, but not for much longer as a staple here. It is an uneasy time, trying to strike the balance between ripeness and rain.

Every bush in the garden has been eaten bare by migrating flocks, as they build up their strength. Red currants and blackcurrants are gone, and the gooseberries picked clean, except for a meagre pound or two, which I made into jam. It is my own fault, forgetting to cover the bushes with netting. This year I only dug part of the garden, but the parsley is dark green, lush and full of flavour, the carrots small and sweet, cabbages big-hearted, and thyme and chives have flavoured many meals. Mint crops up everywhere, but I love it and don't resent its prodigality. Even the marigolds and nasturtiums are still in bloom, gloriously orange and red among the rows of lettuce.

This warm summer and autumn have given us bunches of sweet-smelling roses from the old Jacobite rose, planted long ago by Tommy's great granny. Even the ancient pink roses in the deserted garden have flourished, close-petalled and full of scent. The bees have had long hot days to ransack the fuchsia and escallonia, but they seem to love the purple hebe best. I love standing close to the old gnarled bush, covered in bloom, and alive with the buzzing of bees. It is the essence of summer. I have never been stung, they ignore me. Bunches of pungent tansy and apple ringie hang in the airing cupboard to deter moths.

Grass of Parnassus is still growing in the wetlands along the shore of the loch, and clustering around the old lichened march stones. They are larger and more numerous than usual, with translucent petals striped with green. The watermint is in purple bloom, and scents the air with its elusive fragrance. Pink and white ragged robin is in flower and lady's bedstraw, yellow among the white clover. Nowhere is the honey-scented pink clover, which used to line the verges and fill the fields. Modern grass seed must have rid itself of the children's 'curly dodos'.

Often this year I have walked along the inside of the dyke instead of on the shore, and have found many wild gardens which I have never seen before. Near the 'Heavenly Quoy', a field from which only the blue sky can be seen, there is a fresh-water ditch, full of a riot of blue forget-me-nots, with yellow iris growing along the edges. Watercress floats in the stream, and sheets of orchids and lady's smock are in hollows sheltered from the wind. It is a lonely place, silent except for the gulls wheeling and calling, and the seals singing in the bay. Only the occasional bird watcher wanders along the shore, hoping to be the first to spot a rarity.

Everything is in a hurry now, a feeling of restlessness to finish the harvest, get the byres ready, fences repaired since the equinox brought the change in wind and sea, and the darkness will be back, and the sunny days become a memory. Already the stars can be seen, and the harvest moon sails huge and peaceful above the sea, shedding her calm light on flagstone roofs and quiet fields.

The Swedish connection

THIRTEEN years ago, our daughter Caroline, then ten years old, sent a letter to *Farmers Weekly*, with a drawing of our Manx cat, Tabitha. All four children signed the letter, and since at that time no newspapers except *The Orcadian* came to North Ronaldsay, it disappeared without trace. Then, only a week or two later, a letter arrived from Lisbeth Ing-Marie Persson, who owned three Manx cats, and was also one of four children on a farm in Sweden.

For the children here to get a letter from Scandinavia was very exciting. Everyone in both families joined in, and we found that we had more and more in common. Three of their four children were very close in age to ours, and the two youngest boys, who were four and five years old, exchanged drawings. Lisbeth even shared her name and age with our Mary Elizabeth. Lisbeth's mother, Berit, and I began to exchange letters every fortnight, Berit in Swedish, and I in English.

It's hard to describe the feeling of liberation this friendship has brought us. It has opened up a whole new world, as well as teaching us a new and beautiful language. We started a large scrapbook, and exchanged photographs of everyone, of birthdays and confirmations, the day Lisbeth won an enormous teddy bear at the fair, making silage and hay, cutting down trees in the forest, playing on the beach, our daily lives were recorded and put into scrapbooks.

Lisbeth and her mother came to stay with us, and we were soon good friends. We share recipes and exchange seeds, make tapes for each other, and talk on the telephone. One of the best Christmas presents we have ever had has been a set of decilitre measuring spoons, so that we can bake gingerbread cookies, as well as bread and other things. All our Christmas decorations are from Sweden, plaited straw with red ribbons, and we also have traditional wall-hangings of angels and candles. Our bread boards and butter knives are wooden, and Lisbeth's grandfather made us a bowl of turned beechwood, which is used all the time for holding apples.

We have Berit's woven tapestries on the walls, and through her I have learned all sorts of handwork, especially counted cross-stitch. We exchange patterns of all kinds, and weekly magazines, hand-dyed wool, and home-spun wool. This friendship has taught me so many skills, and also a great deal about food and nutrition, because Sweden is in the forefront in educating people about health care. Years before there was any publicity about additives in this country, they were banned in Sweden.

In May we were invited to Lisbeth's wedding, and Mary and I went together. The farm is in Skone, among gently rolling hills and valleys, and everywhere the trees were in blossom – apple, pear, cherry, lilac, fragrant, drifting clouds of petals. The ground was carpeted with lily of the valley, growing up out of last year's leaves. Solbacken is a dairy farm, and it was so interesting to see the cows and calves, and go with them to fresh pastures. There are still three Manx cats, and swallows nest under the red roof of the white farmhouse. Behind the farm there are tall birch trees, making a cool green shade.

On the wedding-day, the flag was flown from the flagpole in the garden. Berit picked white narcissi for the altar, and tulips, and we went to see the church in the morning, with paintings of flowers and leaves in its peaceful eleventh century interior. It must have seen years of desperate famine and poverty, as well as good harvests, marriages, baptisms and confirmations.

A Swedish bride isn't given away by her father. The couple walk up the aisle together, preceded by a small flower girl in white. Lisbeth was a beautiful bride, as she stood beside Jan under an arch of green leaves and tulips. When the marriage was over, they drove away in a carriage drawn by two grey horses, in the warm evening sunshine, to an inn six miles away. Horses in the fields came galloping down to whinny at the carriage horses trotting past, the birds sang, and the bells were ringing. The old inn was flying the Swedish flag, and inside there was a low, beamed ceiling, and a wooden floor, embroidered pictures and woven tapestries, and oil lamps on the white walls. The meal was delicious, and afterwards there was dancing, and coffee and liqueurs, and wedding cake.

The moon was high in the sky when we left to go home, and nightingales were singing in the cool half-light. A larger-than-life size wooden stork had been fixed on the barn roof, so that it could be seen for miles around.

The rest of our holiday passed far too quickly. We gathered birch leaves, and were shown how to dye wool, and visited the rose-pink palace of Christinehof. Berit wore her Albo district dress, with its hand-woven striped apron, and honeycombed arm bands, and monogram. We saw old farmhouses which had been the home of the poor, and a splendid watermill in action. We drove through the forest and met wild pigs coming back from a roll in the mud. We walked in the fields in the evening sun, and picked lilies of the valley, drank coffee, and laughed, and hunted down fugitive words in the dictionaries.

More than anything else, we enjoyed the friendship which grows deeper with the years, through many joys and problems, and is a bond of affection which transcends language and nationality. There is such a strong bond in Orkney with Scandinavia, and even today, many words in daily use in North Ronaldsay are still the same in Norway and Sweden. It was hard to say goodbye without tears, but we have so many memories which we will always keep, of the kindness and hospitality of everyone we met, of the sunny Swedish springtime with all its blossom, and of the happy wedding day we all celebrated together as one family.

Lace trimmings

I have been washing and ironing a fascinating collection of clothes dating from mid-Victorian times to the twenties. All of them have been looked after very carefully, put away in laundered white cotton bags, in wooden kists lined with newspapers, folded tissue paper, and mothballs. Most articles have never been worn.

The oldest item is a beaded bonnet, complete with artificial flowers and two ribbons, the style worn when women had their hair parted in the middle, very small and neat. There is a short embossed velvet cloak, and long matching skirt, and several long cloaks and coats in heavy dark wool, thick and warm.

Some of the long skirts are especially attractive, with tucks and neat waistbands. There are tailored jackets with leg o' mutton sleeves, and braid trimming, in black on sage green. All are home-made, with excellent shaping, and lined throughout.

By far the prettiest clothes are the long white cotton petticoats, with yards of broderie anglaise flounces, all hand sewn and tied with tapes, or ribbons. They are all tailored to fit at the waist, without gathers. Some of the petticoats are navy and white striped, with a bias frill. One is rose-pink cotton and white lace, and there are warm white flannel ones, with scalloped hems, for winter, as well as pink and white crocheted petticoats, and red flannel. I like the chemises, or sarks, with their delicate pin-tucked yokes, and insertions of yellow or blue ribbon. The cap sleeves are edged with broderie anglaise. Several are plain pink and blue striped flannel, all still in their original folds, never worn since they were made. There are bodices with long and short sleeves, with neatly shaped backs, hand-sewn button holes, and lace trimmings along the fastenings and cuffs. Some are very small, and would have fitted a little girl of eight or nine. The school pinafores of plain white linen, with bib and long ties, and frilly cotton ones, are very attractive, and there is a pink one with deep pockets, trimmed with flowery pink braid.

Most interesting of all are the Edwardian blouses, high-necked and long-sleeved, both made at home and bought. They are mostly elaborate, with bands of tucks and lace insertions, long cuffs and pearl buttons, and full sleeves. They are made in a variety of materials, cotton lawn, pure silk, and voile. With the blouses are embroidered collars, mostly square, in fine silk material, as fresh and pretty as the day they were bought. The lace collars are interesting to look at, pressed and pinned on to a dark background. The patterns are intricate, flowers, stars, ladders, spiders' webs and lovers knots.

There are yards of fragile trimmings for underwear and pillow cases. Some have been sewn on, then unpicked and washed for re-use. There are also pink and blue silk sashes, too far perished to wash, and pairs of unworn white gloves, still joined at the wrist.

As time went on, the clothes became simpler. There is a brown dress from the twenties, with a darker brown floral trim, in a very fine thin material, never out of its packet. In its original hat box, complete with its receipt for 6/11d, is a blue hat with dark blue ribbon, from J. and R. Allan's dated 1927.

It's fascinating to take care of these things from long ago, to put them safely away, for so much skill went into making them. Certainly no-one here now would have such elaborate and feminine blouses and lace. It's interesting to think of all these Edwardian girls wearing their frilly white blouses, and ankle-length skirts, over flouncy petticoats, waists nipped in by boned stays, and silver-buckled belts, black button boots over fine knitted stockings, and their long hair pinned up, going to church on Sundays.

Summer solstice

ON midsummer eve we thought it would be fun to have a look at the standing stone, to see if it had any special significance at the summer solstice. It was a cold, damp night, with hazy horizons, and the stone looks particularly unearthly in such weather, brooding alone in a wide and empty field.

It is about ten or twelve feet tall, and there must be as much under the ground, to fix it so rigidly. I wonder how the ancient people went about choosing their sacred stones, whether it was some feature intrinsic to that particular stone, or whether they fixed on it because it was a suitable size and shape, sanctified later by sacrifices and rituals. This stone has a hole big enough for a human hand to go through, high up. It is packed down on either side by stones set in edgeways.

We have never seen it so late at night, and it was eerie listening to the silence, just the startled corncrakes and lapwings flying up into the air, the soft scud of rabbits' feet, and the sea lapping against the pier, and giggling children in the dusk.

The top half of the stone is thickly covered in lichen, but the lower half has been kept smooth by generations of cattle scratching their backs against it. There is an amazing view in every direction, over the firth to all the north isles, which is why this site must have been chosen. In a flat landscape, the stone assumes a stature which it would otherwise lack.

There was no sun to watch setting, and no darkness, for within a few minutes from midnight the sky began to clear, and show patches of light in the north east, behind the lighthouse. We went to see the beams as the light turned slowly, and the swans drifted sleepily on the loch, caught in its rays.

Next day we walked along the white sand of the Nouster Bay, to Burrian Broch, which lies right round the point, overlooking the approaches from south and east. It retains the feeling of a fortress, although it is crumbling into the sea, stone by stone. Part of its double circular wall is still standing, and inside the broch the grass is long and green, beside the deep, stone-walled well. The layers of mortar are being undermined, and there are deep holes going under the turf, full of pieces of bone, crumbling limpet shells, and chips of flinty stone. Clover and sea pinks grow among the stones.

It is a beautiful place, warm and sheltered, and on the rocks below the walls there are deep inlets, and small sandy bays, flat rocks where the cormorants watch, and seals swim in close to the shore. Just beyond the point, a huge colony of seals had come up on to the rocks to dry out in the sun. They were squabbling, pushing each other off the best flat rocks, snorting and snarling, baring their teeth, and shaking the salt water off their long whiskers. It was funny to listen to them singing in their high voices, and coughing and spluttering and sneezing. It seemed to be the elegant slender females who were having mothers' meetings, with their pale speckled pups coming up beside them. The great bull seals were asleep in solitary state, stretched out in the sunshine, occasionally scratching their backs with a lazy flipper.

Fulmars flew low over us, skimming our heads with their wings, dipping and soaring, they are the most graceful of birds in flight. It was a long walk home in the evening sunshine, along the bay, and up past the standing stone, and Holland House, where laburnum drops its golden petals, and the fuchsia bushes are covered in crimson buds.

Birds, bees and rabbits

THE AIR is full of scent from the white clover, which is in bloom everywhere. The washing smells of flowers, when I bring it in from the dyke, and the whole house has a lingering fragrance, drifting in through open windows and doors. This wet July has made everything grow to twice its usual height. The cattle stand in grass up to their middles, trying in vain to eat it down, and when they are lying chewing the cud, or sleeping away the warm afternoon, they are lost in a green sea of waving grasses and golden buttercups.

Deserted gardens are rhubarb jungles, with vast, red trunks and massive umbrella leaves towering a foot above the dykes. We hear the birds in the fields without seeing them. Corncrakes croak in the damp dusk, and young birds practice their calls in strange wheezes and grunts and whistles in the long grass. Only out on the bare short turf, outside the northern dyke, are the hollows of the arctic terns clearly visible, and their fat chicks run about among the rocks, while parents shriek and swoop. A large grey owl was sitting on a fencing post, placidly watching the sights, his astonishingly flexible neck turning in all directions to watch tractors and trucks drive past.

The young rabbits have lured all our cats away, even the pampered silver Manx tabby, reared in idle luxury. All, all have gone, the old, familiar felines. Occasionally we catch glimpses of furry forms flattened on the ground watching burrows, or crossing the road intent on business. The cats do a good job keeping down as many rabbits as they can, but they are increasing very fast in some parts of the island, and they can eat down the fields in a short time. They become quite brazen about their work of destruction, sitting up on hind legs to watch passers-by, not bothering to move, washing their faces with their paws, not forgetting behind the ears.

Wild thyme is growing in many places this year, close to the ground, with small neat leaves and dark pink flowers. Among the clover is a species of trefoil which I haven't noticed before, small bright yellow flowers, and there are great stretches of bird's foot trefoil near the lighthouse, where the rocks come through the grass. Heather grows there too, and vernal squill. Near the school brae is a bank of marguerites, and along the verges by the water pump, there are clumps of bright blue crane's bill. Out on the southern shore there are sheets of self-heal, a plant which grows much larger there than in the colder, more exposed west. The dwarf plants outside the dyke have their own fascination, because of their minute perfection. It is surprising that anything can survive the tundra-like conditions, but they are tenacious, and find shelter behind stones, and in ancient ditches, long dried up.

Every summer there is a kaleidoscope of flowers, colours drifting into each other through the season. Pink herb Robert grows thickly along the path beside the oats, eyebright and stitchwort are everywhere. There are so many bumble bees this summer, buzzing into the furry centres of the irises, blundering against the pink clover. One enormous bee, perhaps a queen, has twice trapped herself between the top and bottom of the sash window in the kitchen, and we have had to get her out quickly, without hurting her. Eventually she was extricated, and flew away, sizzling angrily to herself. These summer days are full of the sound of bees.

I went to pick roses from an old garden, and the bush has grown to a great size, covered in bloom. A blackbird has built a nest among its branches. It must be an old species, dark pink and white flat roses, with a sweet scent, and red leaves. There is another rose bush there, almost hidden, overwhelmed by its more exuberant neighbour. It has much larger flowers, fat roses with layer upon layer of pale pink petals, also scented, and with paler green leaves. But best of all is the white rose bush, for a few rosebuds in a glass scent the whole house. They are shaded from pale pink in the centre, through cream to white, and the thorns are sharp, and wickedly curved. Their time of blooming is short, but every summer they flower without any attention, and all the old houses have this rose bush.

The escallonia has grown to fill a third of the garden, with its sticky pink flowers, and purple veronica, or hebe, rarer here than the white variety, has flourished in neglect, and is full of bees. Ancient shrubs bloom in the shelter of the broken dyke. There is a carpet of stonecrop and house leek, 'cups and saucers', snow in summer, orange and red monkey flowers, granny's bonnets, and pink shamrock. Hypericum grows there, and silver and green archangel.

The garden has gone back to nature so fast, bushes and flowers growing with robust vigour. In spite of its tangle, it has great charm, silent except for the birds, which live there undisturbed by cat or human footstep.

Soon the last of the bale stacks will be finished, the holidays over, and all the visitors gone. The great red moon rises low in the sky, hazy in the mist, but in the early hours of the morning it is so bright that it lights up the rooms, and covers the loch in a net of silver. The stars will be back in a few short weeks, and the honey scent of wet clover will be forgotten for another year.

September song

THE banks of purple vetch have faded, and all along the roadside the clover is turning from creamy white to brown. There are still poppies and forget-me-nots in the oats, and patches of untidy ragwort in the rough ground where no cattle graze. The rose-pink and gold of the summer flowers have vanished in the last few weeks, as the sun begins to sink lower in the sky. Almost overnight, the long grass has gone, the nettles have disappeared, and only the tangled and ravelled fields of oats are left.

So much rain has flattened the crops in many parts of the island that the unripe oats are being cut for silage, instead of being left to ripen, to be cut with the binder and stooked. Times have changed so much that it seems hard to believe how precious each small rig of oats and corn once was, for the household, as well as for the cattle and horses.

A good crop was needed to provide seed corn for next year, as well as for food and fodder. The old school log books are full of entries from the 1800s, saying that hardly any children were attending school, as they were all required to help at home. Reverence for the grain which kept starvation away, and nourished man and beast in good and bad years must be inborn, because it is such a basic part of life, and so much depended on a good crop and safe harvest.

In a few weeks the harvest will be over, and every field bare and empty, the end of another farming year. The birds are gathering everywhere now, wheatears perch on fencing posts and fly down to the garden dyke. Redstarts come in their thousands, sparrows swoop on the oats and strip the grain from the stalks. Soon the wild geese will fly south with their haunting call carried on the wind. This fills me every year with a terrible sense of loss, for another summer gone, with its blue seas and skies, its wild flowers and green grass, and bees, and for everyone who has shared the warm summer days, and like the birds, are going south.

All the native sheep are back outside the dyke, on the shore with their lambs, before the September equinox brings in great swathes of tangles. From now on there will be more and more seaweed for them, for autumn and winter are their best seasons. The supply of food is endless, replenished twice a day by the tides.

At least when the storms come, the risk of autumn fog will be over, the close damp fog which clings round the houses, and covers the ground. The whole island disappears from sight, and only the booming of the foghorn, and the calling of the seals, give any indication that life exists beneath the thick grey wadding that smothers everything. It is worst in the afternoon, when there are only a couple of hours before the airport closes down. We are very lucky to have Loganair coming so regularly, for it is seldom that the planes are stopped by fog for long. The pilots have saved many lives, including mine, and they are a vital part of island life. Without them, doctors, teachers and nurses would not come to work in the islands, and people would leave if there was no doctor. Apart from essential work, like bringing the vet, and the mail, they make life much more pleasant by flying in newspapers and fresh bread, bringing perishables when the steamer is storm-bound, and taking all our children home from school and college.

The harvest moon glows in the night, and shooting stars wheel through infinity, disappearing before we can point them out, bright flashing sparks racing across the sky. The golden days of autumn, with their late sunshine and mist, are blowing past like leaves in the September wind.

The missing shingle

THESE DAYS are full of storms. Over the dyke the seas are pounding Seal Skerry, huge green waves breaking in white spume. Salt spray fills the air, and already all the windows are crusted with white. Hair and skin feel uncomfortable, sticky with salt, and eyes sting in the wind.

No matter how well the stacks are tied down, the gales can rip off the tops, and there is always a struggle at the height of the storm to catch and hold down ropes, and attach them to heavy scrap iron and pitprops. This time a section of dyke came hurtling down while we were tying down, tons of heavy stones crashing into the yard beside us. In the summer it is easy to forget the power of these storms, which whip up the sea into a frenzy.

Flat islands have no escape, for the wind roars straight across, tearing up everything in its path. Upstairs we hear the full force of the gales, which can smash in windows, rip off slates, and blow down television aerials. Caravans have little chance in such a climate, and they can be killers, unless properly wired down in cement, for the gales can blow them right over and take off the roofs.

It is dangerous to go out, even though it is necessary, for you never know when something is going to come flying through the air, or lifted from the ground, or blown off a trailer. Migrating birds are blown wildly off course, often forced down and killed by flying into the lighthouse. Even those which have found some shelter among the low sycamores in Holland gardens must find it hard to survive, when it is difficult for a grown man to walk against the storm.

The pier is frightening in these conditions, for the sea can sweep right over it, and the firth disappears from sight in suffocating and blinding spray. It used to be dreadful when there was no plane, and storms prevented the post boat and steamer from coming to North Ronaldsay. When anyone was ill, it could be a very dangerous trip for the lifeboat, taking many hours to get to and from the island. Sometimes seine netters were called in to take seriously ill people to hospital. Now it can take as little as an hour to reach the intensive care unit in Aberdeen.

Every year there is a massive shift in the beaches round the island. The bay at the pier has lost all its grey shingle, and gone back to its former pure white sand, stretching in a perfect curve right round the south of the island. All summer the seals abandoned it, preferring the rocks beneath the broch, but now they have moved back to the sand, while the sheep move slowly among them, eating the seaweed left by the tide.

The shore below our house has also changed, with hundreds of tons of shingle washed away, and great stones in sight, which have been buried under the sand. They were used long ago to tie boats up, when they were hauled up out of the sea. It is strange to think how many men down the centuries must have used the same stones and anchorage, for their boats. Now there are none left, except one or two small creel boats, *Viola*, *Elizabeth*, *Mary Jane*. The sea can shift vast quantities of sand and shingle in such a short time, totally altering miles of shoreline.

Although it isn't yet cold, we light the downstairs fire every day, and the kitchen range stays on day and night, filling the room with its comforting heat. It is a relief to come in out of the wind, even though the noise is still deafening, and the aerial has blow round, losing the television picture. We can only wait till the storm has blown itself out, and everything calms down again.

Snow and sea and moonlight

WINTER has come to the island, bringing blizzards from the north, piling soft snow half up the doors and windows. Drifts hide the roads, icy traps for the unwary, and smooth white snow covers deep ditches. It is so cold, this whirling fog of snow crystals, powdering faces and jackets, making snowmen of everyone.

Only the cattle are warm and dry, unconcerned at the weather, eating their hay in the low-roofed byres. Pulling out bales, carrying them round to the byres, and mucking out, is a good way to get warm.

The snow came suddenly, freezing the loch again, and changing the leached grass into brittle slivers. The full moon shines so brightly on the snow-covered fields that it is impossible to sleep. The cold, silvery-blue light stretches its icy fingers between the curtains, filling the room with its chilly dream-like glimmer, with moon shadows which float and waver in the cold air. Soft thuds strike the window panes, like the paws of small animals, as a snow shower passes across the moon.

There is no sign of life in this icy world of snow and sea and moonlight. It could be an uninhabited island, for no human footprints mark the fresh snow, and everyone is asleep. No house lights can be seen, except the lamp in the doctor's porch, and the new pier light, which glows so brightly that we can see it behind the school brae, three miles away.

The cats sleep in nests deep inside the stacks. Only the native sheep are awake, for they live by a tidal clock, sleeping, eating, and chewing the cud by the times of the tides. This morning when we went to look for driftwood over the dyke, their hoof-prints were everywhere, making an easy track to follow along the beach. There was a heavy sea running, dark pewter waves, with frothy curling crests, racing up the shingle, and throwing tangle and wrack up on to the tide-line.

Under the dyke the snow had piled up in high drifts, and there were broken fishboxes and branches. There was a snow shower, a storm of snowflakes blown through the salt spray, so that it was impossible to distinguish between driving snow and sea spray. The dyke is slippery to climb over in snow, and we were glad to get back to the house with enough wood for the fire. It's lovely fuel to burn, crackling and sparkling blue and purple and gold as the salt ignites.

In this weather it's good to have plenty of flour, bere meal and oatmeal for bread and bannocks. There is milk and butter, rice and lentils, eggs, cheese and fruit, vegetables, and enough coffee and tea. Just as important is a full tank of oil, to keep the range going, and the water hot. We need paraffin for lamps, in case of a power cut. If there are severe storms, we can't expect the steamer to come, and the roads can be blocked overnight by snow. There is plenty of hay for the cattle, and sacks of potatoes in the shed.

Everyone is thankful for a hot meal, after being outside in driving sleet, when the wind cuts like a wet knife, snow gets down your neck, and people sink up to the knees in drifts.

Now that it getting dark, the blizzards have increased, and it must be impossible to see the road now. It would be too dangerous to try to walk or drive home, so everyone has to be in, cattle work done, before teatime. It would be terrible to be out alone, in the dark, in the drifting snow, with no light to be seen, not even the lighthouse, only the howling of the north wind, and the sea crashing on the rocks below. People could freeze to death in weather like this.

A warm room, enough to eat, and everyone well, and together, is a lot to be thankful for. It will be a relief when the snow disappears again, beautiful and dangerous, taking its icy-cold quilt of smothering down back to the far north.

Lighting candles

THE CATTLE have all been suppered, on this frosty, starry night, when the moon lights the sky like a Christmas lantern, and the frozen grass crunches underfoot. There is always this calm, still time, a time of peace, before Christmas comes rushing through the winter cold.

Every year the same traditions are kept, for nothing must be forgotten, or the fragile and mysterious magic might be diminished. The four candles of advent must be lit one by one at their appointed time, and a candle kept burning in the window, to shine out into the dark of midwinter, a tiny spark in the vastness of night, the symbol of life, and the return of the light.

The lighting of a candle is an ancient ritual, a universal symbol. The first candle of advent brings Christmas to the door of the house, a glowing flame leading the shining procession of lights and scents, of pine and spices, cinnamon and cloves, and carols and bells, and memories of other years.

The northern countries believed at one time that the dead returned to their homes at this time. The man who ploughed the land knew that an endless line of forefathers had cultivated the same soil, each giving his life to the land, and that he followed in their footsteps. The wife who spun her wool, wove, and baked the bread which nourished the family, knew that an endless chain of women before her had done the same thing in the same place, in an unbroken continuity, each one lighting a candle for the next generation.

It was thought that they all shared a longing to return to the hearth where they had lived their lives on earth. Food and drink was set out, and a light left burning, and the family went discreetly to bed, to avoid meeting their guests. Later on, the custom was Christianised, the candle left burning to light the holy family to Bethlehem, or to welcome the Christ-child to the home. Whatever the ancient belief, it is a beautiful and good tradition, and the warm glow of candlelight shines in the dark of the northern night.

The stars fill the sky with an icy glitter, so far away that the island seems even smaller, an obscure rock in a cold and turbulent sea. The moonlight moves on the waves, and over the loch, and the lighthouse beam sweeps over the farm buildings and houses.

This year I was mixing the Christmas cake when the swans flew over with a rhythmic rush of wings, necks outstretched, calling to each other on the wind. Some are cygnets, but there are several full-grown swans in their white plumage, with bright orange beaks. They are the most graceful of birds, a fascinating and inseparable part of life on the island, returning through countless centuries, by the same strange instinct which brings them back to the same small loch, generation after generation.

We hear the sound of their flight, and their wild

calling, as they fly below the shining constellations to land on the loch, and in the first pale green light of dawn there is the splashing of water, as they take off, one after another.

Christmas is full of simplicity here. The byres are warm and peaceful, and the cows munch their summer-scented hay, and chew the cud. They are comfortable and contented to be out of the cold and dark. The kitchen is filled with the scent of an orange stuck with cloves, and with winter jasmine, just coming into flower, its white petals a drift of fragrance.

The Christmas puddings boil on the range, beside the kettle, and driftwood is drying beside the oven. The grey tabby is purring by the fire, after his morning hunt through the frozen reeds on the other side of the loch, and his irresponsible bound across the ice, when he heard the back door open. Daylight is short now, with dusk coming in the afternoon, and the first star shining soon after four.

Not so long ago, the yule sheep and the brewing of ale were the vital parts of Christmas, and some of the traditions must have been from the distant viking past, for Scandinavia retains many of the customs once common in the northern isles. The power of the new and waxing moon was vital for the slaughtering of the pig, and the Christmas baking had to be done at the same propitious time.

Care had to be taken to put the ladle into the porridge pot before it came to the table, because the first person to make a hole in the porridge would die in the coming year. The house had to be specially clean, and also the occupants, and something new was worn to keep away evil. Cattle and horses were given an extra good feed, and a sheaf hoisted on a pole for the birds.

Now there are few rituals to observe, but the Christmas candles always shine out in the dark, to remind us of the coming of light, the return of the sun, and the triumph of life over death.